Men of the Kingdom

John Knox: The Reformer

By

ISAAC CROOK, LL. D.

Author of " Jonathan Edwards " and
" The Earnest Expectation."

CINCINNATI: JENNINGS AND GRAHAM
NEW YORK, EATON AND MAINS

Dedication

———

To the wife of my youth,

DEARER AS THE YEARS GO BY, WHOSE SKILLFUL CARE
HAS PRESERVED MY HEALTH, WHOSE INTELLIGENT
HELP IN RESEARCH, AND WHOSE FINE DIS-
CRIMINATION, HAS GREATLY AS-
SISTED IN THIS BOOK.

Sentiments from Knox

"Above all things, preserve the kirk from the universities."

"If princes exceed their bounds, no doubt they may be resisted even by power."

"God subjects people under princes, and causes obedience to be given under them."

"God forbid that I ever take upon me to set subjects at liberty to do whatever pleases them."

"I have learned plainly and boldly to call wickedness by its own name—a fig a fig, and a spade a spade."

"Man always thinks he can derive a more perfect honoring of God than that which He Himself hath commanded."

"There has been and shall be, even to the coming of the Lord Jesus, a Church which is holy and universal; to wit, The Communion of Saints."

"What I have been to my country, albeit this unthankful age will not know, yet the ages to come will be compelled to bear witness to the truth."

"I see the steeple of that place where God first in public opened my mouth to His glory, and I am fully persuaded that I shall not depart this life till that my tongue shall glorify His name in the same place."

CONTENTS

Part I

THE MAN AND HIS COUNTRY

Part II

HIS ERA

Part III

MONUMENTS

Part IV

SHAMROCK AND THISTLE

INTRODUCTORY

"BIOGRAPHIES are dull." So is much of history, cyclopedia, and lexicon. The difference is in the method.

This book was started by two sentiments,—one spoken at the grave of Knox by Earl Morton; the other attributed to Knox, which I can not verify. Both will appear toward the end of this volume.

The task of Knox was the most difficult of the famous Reformers, and completest done. Iconoclast, of necessity; but chiefly Reformer.

Knox is the most conspicuous character in Scottish history. The facts will appear in this book.

What is he to us in America? His people and principles, like live wires, penetrate life all about us.

Most histories and biographies "lippen" so hard to favorite men, nations, and forms of faith, as to depreciate those contrasted. This is a sure way to be unreliable, do injustice, and present false views, not only of those criticised, but also of the subject of eulogy. Much of the writings concerning Knox and his times is thus vitiated. Difficult as is this task, we hope to have succeeded fairly well.

Protestants are not all good; neither are Roman Catholics all bad.

It were bigotry to despise men like John Henry Newman, leading the world in singing "Lead, Kindly Light," or Bernard of Clairvaux, author of such songs as "Jesus, the very thought of Thee;" or Bernard of Cluny, singing "Jerusalem the Golden;" or saints like Fénelon, with his intense love of moral duty; Thomas Aquinas, the "Angelic Doctor;" or Thomas à Kempis, with his "Imitation of Christ." It has remained to our day for Protestant lecturers to exalt the moral hero Savonarola. We pity, while admiring, the late Archbishop Elder, appealing to Mary in his dying breath.

There is an archbishop in the Northwest, and a cardinal in the East, a brilliant patriotic pair, who, though hampered, stand for righteousness.

Books are usually written for the author's fellow-countrymen. This is seen in the many assumptions and implications leaving to the reader who lives in other lands the task of interpretation. This is troublesome if he has a large library; and if not, he is helpless.

Foreign writers leave untranslated their phrases, currency, revolutions, order of sovereigns, greatly to the dissatisfaction of readers of a different nationality. This may account for some of the simplifications attempted in this book.

We hope to be fair when we enter the storm-center of the Scotch Reformation as it swirled round Mary, Queen of Scots. Many historians have acted simply as her apologists, discounting, and even denouncing, all who assisted in rescuing Scotland from the ruin certain to have come had she prevailed. She was not to blame for her hot blood, great cunning, intense selfishness, nor for having been thrust before the world as a child of six, and placed under the training of Catherine de' Medici. Neither can her faults be condoned without sympathy with sin. She broke away, and in two years dashed through a sluice of moral corruption from Darnley to Bothwell, and into a twenty years' imprisonment, ended by being beheaded.

In the preparation of this book I have sought information in history, biography, theology, and fiction, ancient and modern, written by men of different nationalities, friendly and unfriendly toward Knox, as well as what the Reformer himself wrote.

I have corresponded with a wide circle of the

best informed of Scotch and American readers and writers; have looked about among the Scotch and Scotch-Irish Americans, drawing on their traditions, very rich and surprising; have read the proceedings of Scotch-Irish Congresses, being privileged to attend one held in Louisville, Kentucky. While acknowledging my indebtedness to their enlightening and eloquent addresses, I have, in a few instances, returned the "Scotch verdict" on some of their claims to men and measures. I hope, however, to have drawn the Reformer out of a cloudy past into clear modern vision.

PART I

THE MAN AND HIS COUNTRY

CHAPTER I.

"A MAN-CHILD WAS BORN."

FOUR hundred and one years ago, February 28th, seventeen miles northeast of Edinburgh, in a plain Scotch home at Haddington, a child was born and they named him John; a fashionable name at that time, as well as through all the Christian centuries. When this child became a man, and one of the greatest tasks of his life was assigned him, he was placed on a committee of six, every man named John, but his was the dominant mind. Out of that committee, in 1560, came the Scottish nation, with its Kirk, its Confession, and civil liberty. Nor was its Confession Johannean, but rather Pauline.

The father of John Knox was of the upper-middle class, being a somewhat thrifty tenant of the Earl of Bothwell. As this name was but a title, not indicating blood relation, it saves us from supposing that he was like in character to the talented wretch, James Hepburn, who figured later, in the history of Mary, Queen of Scots, as Earl Bothwell.

The Scotch pine, like its species all about the world, grows on high places, often on heights of 2,700 feet; then it shoots skyward for one hundred and fifty feet more. It will live for four hundred years. One would like to find some tree in the Pentland hills yet living climbed or prayed under by the boy Knox.

The tall tree catches the eye, but mere conspicuousness and merit are not identical. Some, like Guiteau and Judas Iscariot, are conspicuous because bad; others like Beau Nash and Darnley, were prominent, but fools. Men like our hero are prominent in spite of themselves.

Hamilton, the martyr; Sir William Hamilton, the philosopher; Wishart, the tutor of Knox, Buchanan, and Andrew Melville, who carried on the reform against prelacy, were jewels as fine or even finer than Knox, but were not so conspicuous.

The inconspicuous man may be so from lack of gifts, graces, or usefulness; or, possessing all these even more than many who are conspicuous, may belong to the least of the kingdom who are its greatest. The world needs more attention to God's jewels after the ideals of George Macdonald in

"Annals of a Quiet Neighborhood," or Legh Richmond with his "Dairyman's Daughter." The rarest fossils and the brightest diamonds are not in the coarse granite peaks on the mountain-top. The two mites of the widow outshine the ostentatious gift of the millionaire. Not so much for himself, but for what he stood, we try to bring Knox out of the shadows of four hundred years. As we shall see, he became conspicuous against his choice.

"THE OUTWARD MAN."

There are half a dozen uncertain, inferior pictures of him, sufficiently contradictory to prove them unreliable. But these are helped out in a written description by Sir Peter Young, tutor of James VI, and sent to Theodore Beza in 1579. By aid of this description, the pictures, and what we know of Scottish habits at that date, there comes before the mind the vision of a man with a Scotch bonnet, covering a head of black hair; with heavy, jutting eyebrows; deepset, large eyes, bluish-gray, bright and penetrating, with a twinkle of humor; a nose prominent, long, somewhat aquiline; a mouth of generous size, and a beard over a foot long. Full beards were then fashionable. He never ate with a fork so as to be embarrassed with that beard, for

2

forks were not in use. His shoulders were broad and his frame was well knit and vigorous before his terrible sufferings as a slave in French galleys, with the added drain of his strenuous life. But he was under size, contrary to what we might imagine from the Scotch type, which no doubt misled the author of the "Queen's Quare," to describe him as a man of large and powerful frame. In stature he reminds us of other great heroes of small frame. Such was Ignatius Loyola, whose zeal sent him about the world to propagate virulent, violent, cruel fanaticism. John Calvin, the leader of the most persistent doctrinal reform of any age, was also small in stature. John Wesley, leader of the greatest revival up to his time, was less than one hundred and twenty-five pounds weight.

These men had much in common,—self-forgetful zeal, fearless aggressiveness, and unconquerable efficiency. Loyola, as a young soldier steeped in vice, being wounded at Pampeluna by a cannon ball, was converted to Romanism and undertook to check the Reformation. Calvin turned away from law and literature to Protestant Christianity. Knox, bred to the Catholic priesthood, was converted, and "cast anchor" in Christ's prayer recorded in John's seventeenth chapter.

The face of Knox appeals to one, both on account of what it is and because of its reflection of his lack-luster life, shadowed, it may be, by something from his ancestors, with a thousand years of feudal strife. It strongly hints a Swiss or French rather than a Scotch face.

It is doubtful whether we should be drawn closely to the wearer of it, reflecting so somber a spirit. Luther might have repelled by a brusque self-assertiveness running over into jollity, while Knox would form but very few friendships like that of Jonathan and David, or that with his own beloved leader, George Wishart, whom he desired to follow to martyrdom at the stake. Though small of stature, it was forgotten as he rose in commanding moral grandeur before crowds, over whom his eloquence swept like the floods from beneath the snows of his native land.

BIOGRAPHY.

This is the soul of history. Let its outline be brief. Knox spent his first seventeen years at home and at school in Haddington; the next eight years in Glasgow University. He spent sixteen years obscurely as tutor in the families of Douglas and Cockburn, also partly employed in the work of a

priest. At the age of forty he became a follower
of George Wishart, who was burnt by the order of
Cardinal Beaton. At forty-one he was called to
preach the Reform doctrines. For two years nearly
he was a galley slave on the "Notre Dame"—trav-
esty on the name!—navigating the French rivers
Seine and Loire. He was very silent about that experience, like the victims of Andersonville prison
in our Civil War. It was too horrible to recall.
For four years after his liberation he preached in
England. Five years he spent, partly in Frank-
fort-on-the-Main; then three years in Geneva as
pastor of a congregation. The last thirteen years
of his life he was in Scotland, finishing the completest Reformation of any in Europe.

He died at the age of sixty-seven. Calvin died
at the age of fifty-five; Luther at the age of sixty-
three; Loyola at the age of sixty-six; but it would
have been disgraceful to die at any such age in
"Drumtochty." He was the father of two sons in
union with Mary Bowes, Nathaniel and Eliezar.
Both were well cared for and liberally educated, but
died early, and left no children. One became a
clergyman of the Church of England. There were
three daughters born of the second marriage; they
became remarkable women. Through them have

descended many of Knox's living posterity, some of whom are found in America.

"THE WHIMPERING SCHOOLBOY."

Knox's father was sufficiently thrifty and wise to afford the lad ample education; first at Haddington, the shire town of the county in which he was born. Some biographies say he went thence to the University of St. Andrews; but most agree in sending him to Glasgow, where he took his Bachelor's degree. One says he took his Master's degree at St. Andrews, where for a time he served as tutor. The disagreement suggests,—

> " Seven cities now contend for Homer dead,
>   Through which the living Homer begged his bread."

In his education he was devoted to the Romish priesthood, then the Church in Scotland. One of his teachers was John Major, a remarkable man, who acquainted young Knox with the learning of the Renaissance. This learning was inimical to the papacy, being a reversal to an earlier independence of thought. It not only awakened a love of literature, but also of logic. It involved the spirit of democracy. Knox was an apt learner, and competed in ability as a dialectician with Major himself.

Both little dreamed of the harvest to come out of this seed-sowing.

After his ordination to the priesthood, which had a secular side, conferring the privileges of civil notary, he entered upon his work as tutor. The families in which he served were Protestant in their leanings. The leaven was quietly at work, until he became a devoted follower of George Wishart, who, on his way to the stake, turned Knox back to his "bairns"—his pupils. It has been a question whether Knox was a great scholar; whether he could rank with Luther, Calvin, Melanchthon, or Zwingli. We shall return to this question further on.

CHAPTER II.

"CALEDONIA."

To UNDERSTAND a man we must consider his native country. Scotland is small. "From Maiden Kirk to John o'Groat's," south to north, it is less than three hundred miles; from east to west, in places thirty, and in others a hundred and forty; from Aberdeen east on the German Ocean to the Isle of Skye on the west, one hundred and fifty. Its thirty thousand square miles could lie down on Ohio with eleven thousand square miles as a spare margin. So are other great countries small. Greece is five thousand square miles less than Scotland, and yet has been felt in the history of the world. The Netherlands conquered by the tireless Dutch, from swamp and sea, the scene for the battle of Puritanism for eighty years, is but thirteen thousand square miles; while Palestine, the pivot of the world's history, is not half as large as Scotland, being only ten thousand square miles. Humanly speaking, it produced the Son of man.

From an airship a sail across Scotland would reveal a wonderful land with a marvelous history. It is surrounded with eight hundred islands and a multitude of deep bays, many firths, entering the German Ocean on the east and the Atlantic Ocean on the west. These rivers spring from wild gorges in the Grampians, dashing through into lakelets and great lochs, drawing to their shores wondering visitors from all lands; around which lakes are trimmings of evergreens, and over which hangs a charm of history, poetry, and romance. The air-voyager would behold the Grampian Hills, in two chains winding mainly from the east, northward and westward, dividing the whole country into two glorious valleys, and themselves terminating in such great captains as Ben Lomond and Ben Nevis. Below him would be much of the time a murky sky, discharging mist and rain, and heavy snows in winter. Above him would be the marvelous blue heavens, so exhilarating to Scotland when the clouds roll away. And still below the mists lie long stretches of plains, reaching from the rivers' brink by way of peat bogs, upward through barren-looking heather-plains, where herds of Highland cattle and flocks of black-faced sheep graze. The rocks are numerous in kind and great in quantity, including paleozoic schist, quartz, gneiss, granite, volcanic rock, coal, iron, and gold, formerly in paying quantities. The voyager would catch glimpses of many old historic castles, monuments of centuries of strife, rapine, luxury, and growth.

Though so far north, lying between near 54° and 58°, the climate is more equal than many similar latitudes. The thermometer is rarely down to zero and seldom up to 80°, with a mean of forty-seven degrees.

It is such a country as to develop a people like the Scotch, and bring out the Wallace, the Bruce, and the grander hero, John Knox.

> " The thistle's purple bonnet,
> And the bonnie heather-bell."

Before we study the task of John Knox, let us look further at the man.

Had this serious-faced hero any sense of humor? Unfortunate the man with heroic work on hands destitute of it. It may be excessive and impertinent and thus weaken a man's power. But Knox

would not have been an all-around Scotchman with
no humorous side. In this the Scotch people differ
somewhat from other nations. The Irish run
strongly to a sparkling wit, which snaps and
startles, but seldom hurts. The German is a little
slow-footed in his humor, and expends it largely
within domestic circles. The American, though in
some sense a combination of all, runs to burlesque
through a race of men extending from Sam Slick,
the clock peddler, to "Innocents Abroad," while
there are those living whose sweet, pure, brilliant
books promise that the race of American humorists
will not soon die out. With the Scotch it resembles
very much their national emblem, the thistle,—sly
and keen without, but sweet and beautiful within.

When Sir Walter Scott grimly tells us that Old
Mortality, during his eighty-six years, grew merry
twice in his life, one would like to have caught the
gleam in the eye of Sir Walter. "Scotch-Irish
John" was asked, by Charles the Bald, the difference between a Scot and a sot. "Nothing, please
your Majesty, except the table." Crockett, in his
description of the session of the Marrow Kirk
Synod, "the only true witnessing and faithful Kirk
of Scotland," pictures the assembly as consisting of

moderator, clerk, and officer. Charges are to be preferred against Ralph Peden; the session is to be private; the officer is commanded to remove all visitors, whereupon said officer removes himself very reluctantly from the hall. The clerk is ordered to call upon himself to present the complaints against Ralph Peden. It is solemnly done. He sits down, and then arises as complainant to read the charges. For some lack of severity, he is reprimanded, and finally expelled from the assembly by the moderator. The clerk in turn assumes to be the assembly itself, and unanimously votes to expel the moderator, and the eavesdropping officer goes wailing down the street, proclaiming that the Marrow Kirk of Scotland is no more. As a specimen of humor in practice, what is better than that of Professor Blackie with his class? On the bulletin board of the university was written the statement, "Professor Blackie will meet his classes to-day." Some student erased the initial "c." The professor, about to pass into the lecture-room, observed that he was to lecture to lasses. He promptly amended the matter by erasing the letter "l," and the students followed in that character. The Scotch-Irish of this country claim Abraham Lincoln as of their blood.

One should like to believe it, for that humor of his which played among the clouds of that saddest, greatest conflict of time is of the same strain with Scottish humor.

Had John Knox any of this? He needed it to illuminate the storm-clouds that hung over his career. He did not run much to qualities aside from those needed for his one work, and he was, therefore, not rounded out to the fullest measure of his capabilities; but we see flashes occasionally of this very serviceable and very human quality.

When chained to the oar of the French galley, a painted image of the Virgin Mary was presented to him to be kissed. This he declined to do, but seizing it remarked, "Lat aur Ladie now save hersel'; she is lycht enoughe, lat her learn to swyme;" and he tossed it into the river. After preaching in Perth against the idolatry of the mass, there followed a riot which resulted in destroying the decorations of the cathedral, and of many other Roman Catholic buildings. Knox blamed it on the "rascal multitude;" he also remarked that they had "destroyed the rookeries lest the rooks might return."

At one of his interviews with Mary, Queen of Scots, she grew angry, and he was obliged to wait in the hall without, in the presence of her four maids. He pleasantly remarked to them, "O, fair ladies, how pleasing were this life of yours if it should abide, and then in the end that we might pass to heaven with all this gay gear; but fie upon that knave, Death, that will come whether we will or not; and when he has laid on his arrest, the foul worms will be busy with this flesh, be it never so fair and tender, and the silly soul, I fear, shall be so feeble that it can neither carry with it gold, garnishing, targeting, pearl, nor precious stones!" When retiring on another occasion from Mary's presence, he overheard men in waiting say, "He is not affrayed." His reply was: "Why should the pleasing face of a gentle woman affray me? I have looked into the face of angry men, and yet have not been affrayed above measure." This was not brag, but the welling up of sub-acid Scotch humor.

Dr. Hume Brown says: "From the Meary bourds with which he enlivens his narrative, we may infer that his daily conversation was not always of justification and predestination, but that he could tell his story and exchange his jest at any time or place where fitting. What distinguished him from men like Calvin and Savonarola is precisely that sense of a humorous side of things which made him at once a great writer and a great leader

of men. Of the value of this quality in the conduct
of human affairs he was himself perfectly conscious,
and deliberately employed it, both in his writings
and in his dealings with his fellows."

"Melancholius ressours," he said in one of his
debates with Lethington, "wald haif sum myrth in-
termixed." Studied anticlimax, grim irony, humorous exaggeration, are as distinctly his characteris-
tics as they are those of Carlyle, in whom also these
are relieving qualities from narrow intensity and an
overbearing temper.

With humor is usually found pity and the power
of pathos; and in Knox more than once his harsh
austerity softens into a mood, the more impressive
that it comes so seldom.

Take an extract from Knox's history describ-
ing a religious row.

"If we interlace merriness with earnest matters,
pardon us, good reader; for the fact is so notable
that it deserveth long memory. The cardinal was
known proud; and Dunbar, Archbishop of Glasgow,
was known a glorious fool; and yet, because he was
called sometimes the king's master, he was chan-
cellor of Scotland. The cardinal comes even this
same year in the end of harvest before, to Glasgow; upon what purpose we omit. Coming forth

(or going in, all is one) at the choir door of Glasgow Kirk, begins striving for state between the two cross bearers, so that from glooming they come to shouldering; from shouldering they go to buffets, and from dry blows to fists and fisticuffs; and then for charity's sake, they cry, 'Disperse it, *dedit pauperibus*,' and essay which of the crosses was finest metal, which staff the strongest, and which bearer could best defend his master's pre-eminence; and, that there should be no superiority on that behalf, to the ground go both crosses. And then began no little fray, but yet a merry game; for rockets were rent, tippets were torn, crowns were knapped, and side-gowns might have been seen wantonly wag from one wall to the other. Many of them lacked beards, and that was the more pity, and therefore could not buckle other by the hair as bold men would have done.

"But fie on the jackmen, that did not their duty; for, had the one part of them re-encountered the other, then had all gone right! But the sanctuary, we suppose, saved the lives of many. How merrily that ever this be written, it was bitter mirth to the cardinal and his court. It was more than irregularity; yea, it might well have been judged 'lèse majeste' to the son of perdition, the pope's own person; and yet the other, in his folly as proud as a peacock, would let the cardinal know that he was a bishop, when the other was but Beaton, before he got Aberbrothock. This annuity was judged mortal and without all hope of reconciliation."

"Go watch the foremost ranks of danger's dark career,
    Be sure the hand most daring there has wiped away a tear."

Had this great Scotchman that tender nature which would move him "to lead about a wife, a sister?" If so, he was endowed with that rich element of Scotch nature, tenderness of sentiment. In this the Scotch are somewhat different from other nationalities. The Italian is open and excessive in his expression of sentiment after the manner of his native sky, flowers, and fruit. The Frenchman is impulsive, exaggerated, and impassioned. In the Scot sentiment swells strong and deep from beneath a cool exterior, after the manner of mountain streams from under the snows and ice of his native land. There is a purity and depth of touch in Scotch song, scarcely matched. It breaks, binds, and blesses the heart. Had Burns been as clean and sober as he was brilliant and tender, he might have eclipsed the poets of the human race with his rare gifts. Had he been as religious as Knox, he might have rivaled Charles Wesley as a writer of hymns. But in that case it is doubtful whether his anniversary had been celebrated yearly.

That wizard of fine English, President Edward Thomson, afterward bishop, wrote in a letter from Europe:

"One says, 'I wish to take advice about a serious matter that weighs on my mind.' 'What is it?' 'Getting married. Is it best?' 'Well, whom have you in view? Is she young, handsome, and virtuous? The sooner you get her, the better. Who is she?' 'O, nobody in particular; it is marrying in the abstract that I am thinking about.' That is young Germany.

" 'Zounds! I love her, and will have her if I have to swim the river for her!' Young America.

" 'No use to deny me or run from me. Where you go, I will go; where you stop, I will stop; where you live, I will live; where you die, I will die; and where you are buried, there will I be buried.' Young Ireland.

" 'She is worth three thousand one hundred and thirty-seven pounds, six shillings, fourpence and half-penny, which, under the circumstances, is not quite sufficient.' Young England."

For the Scotch let me add, She is fairer than a

3

daisy, more beauteous than the bluebell, purer than snow, brighter than Bonnie Doon, satisfying as the morning, gentler than twilight; I love her with my whole heart; for her "I'd gladly lay me doun and dee."

What possibilities of glorious, tender sentiment were beclouded in Thomas Carlyle by his discovery during college days of what he calls, "That villainous thing called a stomach!" A touch of dyspepsia seems to have invaded his moral and intellectual nature. Pure and deep are the streams flowing bright and clear through sunny days and divine beauty from the soul of George Macdonald. Who that has ever made acquaintance with "Rab and His Friends," by Dr. John Brown, but has been compelled to pay the tribute of a tear? Where can be found a more touching story than "Beside the Bonnie Brier-bush," and that glorious "Doctor of the Old School?" This Scotch quality in Knox was mostly spent in impassioned oratory in his attacks on popery and his efforts to save Scotland.

He has been assailed for unfeeling sternness toward women. A book has been written on the subject, and pages of history have been wasted by slurring misrepresentation. There was in his blood something of his Gaelic or Pictish ancestors, who were polygamists, and lived in the dim light of ancient paganism. He lived at a time when much was left for Christianity to do in lifting woman to the level where Jesus placed her. He was doubtless tinctured with the supposed "Pauline" view, and tinged his teaching by ancient rather than modern social conditions. This absurdity lingers yet in some of the Churches. Such was Knox the dogmatic Reformer; but Knox the man was true and tender.

He met woman in four distinct spheres. First, his wrath was aroused against such as Mary of Lorraine; Bloody Mary, with her three hundred murders; Elizabeth, with her talent and duplicity; and with Mary, Queen of Scots, a very Eris of discord. Against such he launched thunderbolts of just wrath, specially in his first blast of the trumpet against "The monstrous regiment [rule] of women."

Another class of women was represented by those converted to Protestantism, harried, and abused by their persecutors. His letters to a group of these, and left to posterity, show him a most tender and sympathizing shepherd and a man who venerated womanhood.

A third test. It is a trite untruth that a mother-in-law is more unendurable than other women. Knox had one with whom to deal. She was a melancholy, repining soul, with morbid conscience. His letters to her show a tenderness and forbearance of the most delicate fondness. As fine a tribute to the Reformer's gentleness as need be found.

A fourth proof of his chivalry is seen in that he was twice married. Nor did his first wife, Mary Bowes when dead, nor her children, fall away from tenderest memories, and the two sons received his unchanging, generous care. His second wife, very young (it was joining sixteen to fifty-nine), was high born, and related to the house of Stewart. It was this wife with whom he communed most intimately during the last week of his life, requesting her frequently to read, and especially the Scripture most sacred to him.

With such an undertone of tender sentiment, he is all the more admirable for having withstood the well-nigh resistless influence of Mary, Queen of Scots. Without rudeness or coarseness, he stood amid the swirling influences about him, like a Scotch granite mountain amid the flood. In the development of our hero we shall trace some of these elements later on.

PART II.
HIS ERA.

CHAPTER I.

REFORMER.

He was one of the world's few conspicuous Reformers. To understand him we must glance at the condition in the world which he confronted and the men he encountered. Of these there were two kinds, favorable and unfavorable.

Yonder in Spain was Philip II. Charles V, weary and sick, had abdicated in favor of Philip. This vain, ambitious, cruel monarch tainted all he touched. Even the Philippine Islands bear not only his name, but his blight. He married Bloody Mary, of England, for the purpose of uniting that country to the scheme of crushing Protestantism from the world. It was his purpose to subjugate France, with the same end in view. Later he sent the Duke of Alva, intending to tear out the heart of brave Holland.

In the time of Knox, France was under those arch-murderers, the Guises, by whose order seventy thousand Protestant French were slaughtered within a week. To this day one looks with horror on the old church-tower of Saint Germaine in Paris, whence the signal for this work of blood rang out. For this slaughter the pope in Rome gave thanks.

Nearer Knox's home, Bloody Mary's work went on in England until she had destroyed more than three hundred martyrs. Succeeding her was the no less incorrigible Elizabeth, willful, cunning, treacherous, unreliable. These Tudor half sisters were daughters of Henry VIII, divorce chieftain of England, characterized by Dickens as a blotch of grease and blood on the page of English history.

Yonder at Rome was Leo X, succeeded by eight more popes in rapid succession during the life of Knox, each with his long finger reaching out to control all the world, Scotland included.

In Scotland he encountered a seemingly hopeless task. The papal Church having universal sway is doubtless well described by the penetrating, wide-eyed Sir Walter Scott, in his romance "The Monastery." He pictures Abbot Boniface as about to surrender his office to his successor. He consoled himself over his fidelity by a review of "Indulgences," "Drinks," "Boiled Almonds," "Improvement of Revenues," "A Curious Screen to Secure from the Northeast Wind." "It cost me no little thought, no common toil, to keep these mighty matters in order." "Barn and bin to be kept full," "Dormitory," "Guest Hall," "Refectory," "Processions," "Confessions;" "I have lain awake for a full hour by the clock thinking how these matters might be ordered."

Though fiction, this was true to life.

It suggests Cardinal Beaton—no fiction—enjoying from his castle window at St. Andrews, a view of the burning of a talented, heroic young man, who had been Knox's spiritual teacher.

McCrea, in his life of Knox, says of the state of the Church in Scotland: "The corruption had grown to a greater height in Scotland than in any other nation within the pale of the Western Church. Superstition and imposition existed in their grossest forms. The clergy obtained exorbitant opulence and power, accompanied with corruption. One-half of the wealth of the nation belonged to the clergy. Bishops and abbots rivaled the nobility in magnificence. They long engrossed the powerful

offices of state. Bishops never preached; they kept
harlots, and bestowed benefices on their sons. The
lives of the clergy were a scandal. Nunneries and
monasteries were the haunts of lewdness and de-
bauchery. The kingdom swarmed with idle, luxur-
ious monks, who, like locusts, devoured the fruits
of the earth."

In undertaking his work as Reformer, there was
a swarm of nobles to be dealt with, half Protestant,
but mercenary in their dealings with civil and religious affairs. They were land-grabbers.

Martyrdom was the reward of dissent in Scotland, and had been so for many a year. Knox's ancestors in the Dark Ages, as Druids, would, of
course, use the argument of torture and fire to secure conformity. In 1407, James Risley was burned
at Glasgow. In 1431 Paul Carew was burned at
St. Andrews—save the saint! In 1494, the Lollards
were scattered and broken. About 1525, Patrick
Hamilton was burned at St. Andrews. Then followed ten more victims. Nineteen years after Hamilton, George Wishart went up through fire. The
last of this illustrious line, John Hill, when over
eighty years of age, was burned. Knox was sentenced to die, but, being absent from the country,

was burned in effigy. In the "John Knox House" in Edinburgh is seen the room where a bullet whizzed past his head. He took his life in his hand when he entered the ranks of the glorious apostles and martyrs.

It may throw a side light upon the situation to remember that when Knox was growing up, so were the cathedrals. For two or three centuries these had sprung up in Italy, at Florence and Milan, and then the largest of all, St. Peter's. Thence they invaded Holland; then to England, where arose Canterbury, Ely, Westminster; while St. Paul's, London, came a century later. This beautiful menace to popular, spiritual life had also invaded Scotland. The now ruined cathedral of St. Andrews was finished nearly three and a half centuries before the birth of Knox. Another one is yet found in Perth, recalling the riot that swept it bare of decoration, after Knox's sermon. There is one at Glasgow, nearly two centuries in building, completed sixty-five years before Knox was born. There is St. Magnus, at Kirkwall, capital of Orkney, twenty-six miles north of John o' Groat's. It was founded in 1137, before the second Crusade. What means it away there off the main land, looking out almost nine centuries over the North Sea? Knox and cathedrals did not harmonize well. Where his views prevailed, cathedrals did not flourish. Far more credit is it that schools and universities have ever followed in his footsteps.

"We are not careful to answer thee, O king!" said the unbending heroes to Nebuchadnezzar. So, in effect, spoke Knox to Mary Queen of Scots and her secretary, who meant his destruction. He had called friends to stand by two citizens arrested in a disturbance concerning the service of mass, which had been outlawed by the Scotch Assembly. The call issued by Knox was regarded by Mary as treason. When, in answer to her summons, she saw him, she laughed, saying, "Yon man made me weep, I will see whether I can make him cry." The Reformer was cool and clear. He proved that he had a right to summon the friends of the Church. The Privy Council before which he stood were seized with a stupor of admiration, and unanimously acquitted him. The queen left the chamber. Lethington, her secretary, was so angry he recalled her, and had the vote taken over. The nobles gave the same vote of acquittal with indignation. That robbed Knox of the martyr's crown.

"THE LION RAMPANT."

This Scottish symbol, with its motto, *"Nemo me impune lacessit,"* is truly descriptive of the people to be reformed. Who were these Scotchmen? One line of ancestry runs back into the dim past more than a thousand years. They were Picts, pagans, polygamists, and fighters as savage and more gifted than the North American Indians. Another line runs back across the channel to Ireland. A thousand years before Knox, these who were the real Scots invaded Caledonia, and gave it the name Scotland. Flodden field, celebrated by Sir Walter Scott in his "Marmion," suggests this stream of history affecting Knox and his times. While he was a boy of eight, the crushing calamity of this battle befell the nation. This, and the death of James IV, turned over the kingdom to his foolish widow, Mary of Lorraine. There were in all six kings of Scotland called James; in them mingled the blood of Robert Bruce and the Stewarts. Marjorie Bruce had married the Lord High Steward of Scotland. The spelling was changed when it became royal from "Steward" to Stewart—by some branches modified to Steuart, or the French-born Stuarts. Thence sprang this gifted, unfortunate race.

Except the sixth, who became James I of England, all these Scotch kings died of violence, either by assassination or in battle. The fourth James crossed the Southern border into England with an army. The Scots were entrapped on a height, and Flodden-field battle strewed the ground with the dead of nearly all the distinguished houses of Scotland. The king fell amidst the fight. With the stories of such battles the boy Knox was familiar. To this day, when the Highland regiments are ordered out, it means a Balaklava, a relief for Lucknow, or a Magersfontein. The skirl of the bagpipe sounding "The Campbells are Coming" sends a shiver through the army. Such material, hard to mold, furnished for Knox his task.

This quality distinguishing them as hard fighters they transferred into the realm of religious warfare. It characterized them during their long history as pagans, afterwards as Roman Catholics, and then as Presbyterian Protestants. After the establishment of the national Kirk of Scotland in 1560, about one hundred years, there came a split among themselves. From this time they divided frequently, mostly to get away from some form of secularism involved in the connection between political and religious matters within the Kirk. Of this cleavage we have a comical illustration in what is now known as the "Wee Kirk," a fragment standing out against the religious spirit of this age tending to union rather than separation. So far it holds on to some fifty millions of property in the name of about thirty ministers and a few hundred members against multiplied thousands of their former brotherhood. Like our hickory, the Scottish Kirk splits easily, but is hard to break. With such timber Knox had to deal.

The most difficult influence within the realm of Scotland which our Reformer confronted was that of Mary, Queen of Scots. It may not be insignificant to note how much this beautiful name, Mary, was then in use. There was Mary of Lorraine, Bloody Mary, Mary, Queen of Scots, with four waiting maids each named Mary. A serpent may have a shining skin.

Knox, coming in contact with Mary's court, had to deal with Bothwell, a cruel, dominating libertine, a very bull of Bashan, and with Darnley, six foot of fool, vain and licentious.

The young queen still spreads discord through history, biography, and fiction. She had the blood of Robert Bruce directly on the maternal side, and that of the house of Stewart in the father's line, and,

added to that, her mother was Mary of Lorraine,
of the family of Guise. Is it any wonder that, with
this triple nature, she could play woman, warrior,
and vixen? She was a diplomat, fascinating, cruel,
and cunning; educated in France, and thus far an
exotic transplanted to Scotland. Her life-work became one of diplomacy, before which all men bent
with one exception, and that man stood amid temp-
est and tide until the day broke—and his name was
Knox.

AN OPEN DOOR.

His task as a Reformer may also be understood
by the openings and helpers as well as the obstacles.

Columbus discovered America thirteen years before the birth of Knox. It was well for this continent and the far reach of his mission that he was
born so soon after the discovery. This will be
clearer later on. When his forerunner, Luther, was
entering a monastery in Germany instead of a law
office, Knox was a child of two years at home in
Haddington. When Erasmus, the Dutch scholar,
first printed the New Testament in Greek, thus
"laying the egg which Luther hatched," Knox
was a lad of eleven years in school at Haddington. When Luther was nailing his Ninety-

five Theses to the church-door in Wittenberg, Knox was a boy of twelve. When Henry VIII chose to play pope in England, Knox was twenty-six years of age, engaged in study. When Ignatius Loyola organized a company of nine persons at Rome for the Jesuit movement, Knox was thirty-two years of age, still in obscurity. When Coverdale translated the Bible into English, Knox, who was to use it as his sword of battle, was thirty-three years of age, yet in papal darkness. When George Wishart returned from the influence of the Reformation in Germany, Knox had reached his fortieth year, and was, by this scholarly leader, brought into the light of Reformation. When Charles V turned the empire over to Philip II, Knox had been out into the light some ten years, nearly two of which had been spent chained to the oars as a galley slave. When the famous "beggars" received their nickname in Holland, Knox was sixty-one years of age, and sixty-two when Alva the butcher arrived in Holland. When St. Bartholomew's massacre took place, the painful news roused Knox to one more tremendous denunciation of papal crime in the year when he died at the age of sixty-seven. Thus by friend and foe, by events

4

favorable and adverse, the door was opened to him in accomplishing the most successful reform of any during the sixteenth century.

SOME JOHN THE BAPTISTS.

There were Reformers before Knox. Luther preceded Calvin. Both were anticipated by Zwingli; he was enlightened by Wyttenbach; Savonarola was before both by a quarter of a century. Jerome and Huss were before Luther's day by a hundred years, their bodies burned and their ashes thrown into the Rhine. Wyclif, though he escaped martyrdom, was, thirty years after his death, honored by having his body burned, the ashes thrown into the Swift, which runs into the Avon, thence into the Severn, and on to the sea. The Albigenses of Southern France were two centuries before Huss and three centuries before Luther. The Waldenses amid the Alps anticipated the Albigenses by half a century. Looking more widely over human history, we are amazed at the persistence of human backsliding, Divine patience, and Reform. They swing back and forth through the centuries like the flow and ebb of the tide. God lost his grip on Adam. Abel was a Reformer. Again, "the heart of man was fully set in him to do evil." Then Noah tried to lead the world back to God. Abraham came out of Chaldea to start a Reform of faith toward Jehovah. Moses led another, to substitute for the Canaanite backsliders a people whose God should be the Lord. The history of the Judges is a repetition of Reformations. The kings and their kingdoms show a series of backslidings and abortive Reformations. The prophets were Reformers. John the Baptist in this was the greatest of them all. The personal ministry of Jesus Christ was a failure as a Jewish Reformation, but the inauguration of a Reform without end.

CHAPTER II.

"THE TWO-EDGED SWORD."

Preacher.

By preaching mainly Knox accomplished his work as Reformer. We shall notice his qualification for this office later on. While yet a Roman Catholic student, he quietly spoke against papal abuses at St. Andrews, and was driven out. As private tutor in the families of two noblemen he was accustomed to hear objections to Church abuses, and gave his consent; but not till the late age of forty-one was he called out as Protestant preacher. The place where this occurred is full of interest. Cross the river Forth from Edinburgh, go thirty-one miles north-easterly, and you will find a promontory looking out on the German Ocean. There is an old city of near seven thousand people, with not much happening, except golf-playing in summer-time. There is a university with two hundred students; Tulloch was but one of its illustrious professors. There are a couple of impressive ruins, the cathedral, which was one hundred and fifty years in building, and a castle, now a desolated old pile. In the cathedral church John Rough, somewhat resembling his own name, officiated as Protestant preacher. Knox was accustomed to attend; as is often the case when the Church is alive, a conviction got abroad among the worshipers that John Knox ought to devote himself to the work of preaching. It was agreed that Rough, during a public service, should declare this conviction and summon Knox to undertake the work. At the close of his sermon, to the astonishment of Knox, he announced the conviction and the summons. Knox was overwhelmed, hesitated, trembled, broke into tears, and retired in confusion to deliberate and pray; for he well knew the tremendous responsibility and the risk involved. In this he reminds us of another prophet who exclaimed, "I am a man of unclean lips;" but in both cases the fire from off the altar touched the lips. Great leaders are reluctant. It is well for the Church and the world if this distinctness of call, in which the Church and Divine providence blend, shall ever continue.

In a few days the Reformer entered the pulpit, and selected for his text the seventh chapter of Daniel, and proceeded to arraign the papacy as the beast described by the prophet. This formed the keynote of the earlier part of his subsequent ministry. Paul's "man of sin" was to Knox, without doubt, the pope. Having thus begun his appeal to the Scripture, he continued relying upon it as the sword of the Spirit. In this he was a model for the pulpit in all time. An ethical gospel is inevitably essential; so must it be educational and reformatory; but Athens went to moral perdition when her art, literature, and logic were at their highest. So Roman law was as the withes on Samson to bind human depravity, and must be so in any age. It was Peter's use of the Scripture, as of the other apostles, that led to the Pentecost. The Dark Ages were dispelled by Wyclif, Luther, and Knox wielding this same sword. It is true that up to the later years of his life he was mainly a prophet of the Old Testament, but denunciation of wrong is far from lacking in the sermons of Peter and of John, the loving disciple. It is the latter who portrays men calling "for rocks and mountains to fall on them and hide them from the wrath of the Lamb and the face of Him who sitteth on the throne." The modern pulpit will never succeed without a sword with two edges, both law and gospel. The preaching of Knox and other Reformers of the sixteenth century, though Scriptural, expended its force very largely in the realm of theory, and very little in that of personal experience. The former quality belongs essentially to the Reformer's calling, the latter to that of the revivalist.

In the Pulpit.

His style of preaching was a combination of intellectual reasoning and powerful oratory. Being a trained dialectician and logician, he took time in preparing the way for application and appeal. It was a day of long sermons, and the people were willing to have it so. As late as the middle of the seventeenth century the Westminster Assembly in London had single prayers lasting two hours, and sermons even longer. They stand for final perseverance.

After Knox had deliberately laid the foundation of his sermon, then came application and appeal, sweeping all before him. James Melville, his devoted student and follower, gives his own experience as a listener at St. Andrews, whither Knox retired from Edinburgh for a time for safety. He says he began at the first of the ser-

mon to take notes, but after awhile was so
thrilled and carried away as to be unable to pro-
ceed with the writing. There is an oft-quoted sentence of Randolph, English ambassador, who, in
writing to Cecil, Lord Secretary of England, de-
clares, "This man puts more life into us in one hour
than six hundred trumpets blustering in our ears."
After Knox's return from Geneva he preached a
sermon in Perth on the idolatry of the mass, which
swept all before him like a storm. An unfortunate
affair followed, in a measure deplored by Knox. A
priest on his way to offer mass jostled against a boy,
who in anger threw a stone. This was followed by a
wild riot; and such was the excited condition of the
great crowd that it stripped the church of its images
and ornaments; nor did this excitement stop at
Perth, but extended to a number of places, and
notably to St. Andrews. In commenting on this,
Knox called the crowd a "rascall multitude," and
remarked that they "destroyed the rookeries that
the rooks might not return."

When the Earl of Murray, to whom Knox was
much attached, had been assassinated, the Reformer's funeral discourse was so moving as to
bring three thousand hardy Scotchmen to tears.
When in later life he became too feeble to enter the

pulpit without help, he would become, during the sermon, so aroused by the sweep of his own earnestness as to look as though he would "ding the pulpit into blads and flee out of it." When his strength was apparently too far gone ever to preach again, the news of the St. Bartholomew massacre reached Scotland. Knox was carried to the pulpit in Edinburgh, whither he had returned from St. Andrews, and again preached an overwhelming discourse, during which he portended the doom awaiting Charles IX, King of France, who had looked on the scene rejoicing. The French ambassador being present in the congregation, Knox personally charged him to bear this judgment to his master. The world is informed of the agony in which the guilty king died, it is said, with the blood exuding from his pores, in fulfillment of the prediction of Knox.

His ability to preach to the more courtly and cultured, if not more intellectual, was proven during his residence in England, after he had been delivered from the French galleys. This was before he unwillingly fled to Geneva from the persecutions of Mary. He was one of the six chaplains to James VI, and was in his turn competent preacher to the most distinguished audience in England.

Knox was a six-sided preacher. When install-

ing his successor he could look back and conscien-
tiously say: "I have preached with a mind void of
hatred against men; my object was to gain them
to the Lord. I never made merchandise of God's
Word, never studied to please men, nor indulged my
own or others' private passions; I sought the edifi-
cation of the Church." These six things he did
as we have seen, with a final appeal to the Word of
God. This weapon he used as the sword of the
Spirit with as much vigor as Peter used his carnal
weapon at the gate of Gethsemane, but with more
discretion.

THE KINGDOM OF HEAVEN SUFFERETH VIOLENCE.

In studying the work of Knox and the Reformers, the question suggests itself, why might not there
have been less of assault and denunciation and more
of personal appeal, thus bringing Reformation
through individual action rather than breaking down
institutions followed by hostilities, often emanating
in war and bloodshed? John Wesley acknowledged
the usefulness of Knox, but deprecated his spirit.
"A calm, even spirit goes through rough work better than a furious one," said he. It is often sug-
gested by Roman Catholics that the Reformation
was on its way, and would have come of itself

within the Church. Over against this stands the fact that reforms and revivals seldom, if ever, come through Councils, with their edicts and plans of campaign.

The history of Catholicism is punctuated with a chain of Councils that have but increased the evils they undertook to correct by decrees, even to the last Ecumenical under Pius IX, which perpetrated the farce of Papal Infallibility. If the way to reform is to ignore the evils of ecclesiastical tyranny, then why are South America, Mexico, and Italy so desperately degenerated after long centuries of unchallenged priestcraft? Had John Knox omitted his denunciations of the papacy, the Reformation would never have come. Standing up against that dark wall encircling him, his method may have been the only one to break through. We are too prone to forget that Jesus, the Lover of the world, used the most terrible language of exposure and denunciation of any prophet of the Old or the New Testament. In this our Reformer walked in the footsteps of Christ. There are abundant samples of this on record. When "Bloody Mary's" marriage was pending, Knox was at Dieppe, where he was sojourning awaiting news from England. He spoke of Mary as "under an English name she beareth a Spanish heart." He personally addressed Gardiner, the Bishop of Winchester, in no very oily terms thus: "O, thou beast, more cruel than any tiger, art thou not ashamed, bloody beast, to betray thy native country? Fearest thou not to open such a door to all iniquity, that the whole of England shall be made a common stew for Spaniards? So wilt thou gratify thy father the devil, and his lieutenant the pope, whom, with all his baggage, thou laborest with tooth and nail to flourish again in England. Why seekest thou the blood of Thomas, Archbishop of Canterbury, of good Father Hugh Latimer, and of that most earnest and discreet man, Dr. Ridley, true Bishop of London?" And much more of this sort, revealing the kind of fearless soul and the gift of plain, scathing vituperation in this Scotch fighter.

He had been in close fellowship and official relation with the rare trio above named. They were men of unusual scholarship, piety, and gentleness. They went to the tower, that grim old castle, together; thence to the common prison in Oxford; thence to the stake in front of Balliol College, and perished in the flames. One can there see their names carved on the same marble shaft, one of England's milestones on her march from savagery toward a lofty Christianity.

It is a mistake to regard Knox in the light of an Old Testament prophet exclusively. As is often the case with strenuous warriors, he mellowed toward the end. His last series of sermons preached in St. Giles, Edinburgh, was on the crucifixion. He intended to follow it with a sermon on the resurrection. His own death came before the sermon, so that he must illustrate the event in his own experience. "At eve it shall be light."

DESTRUCTIVE AND CONSTRUCTIVE REFORMATION.

Reformers are prone to the work of destruction, leaving to others mainly the work of reconstruction. Knox was both, with the emphasis at first upon destruction. Had it not been so, Scotland would have been other than it is. He was not wholly destructive. It was mainly under his influence that in 1560 Scotland was born as a nation; its civil polity established; a confession of faith drawn up and promulgated; public education provided for every Scottish child, with university privileges for every one who would avail himself of them. It was he who sowed the seed of democracy which made the work of Cromwell, eighty years afterwards, possible, out of which came the British House of Commons and before which fled forever the tyrannical assumptions of the Stewarts.

There is often an intimate relation between Reformation and Revolution. This arises largely from the long-lived misunion of civil and religious affairs. It was over a hundred years after Knox before what is known as the Revolution of 1688 occurred. James II, from whom the Jacobite party and name originated, undertook the restoration of the papacy in Great Britain, but under the pretext of toleration. The people rose in revolt, and called his son-in-law, William of Orange, a foreigner, to the throne. Intelligent readers need not be reminded that this was not William the Silent wearing the name of Orange. That splendid hero was assassinated a hundred years before, fighting the battle of Protestantism in Holland. The American Revolution of '76 came eighty-eight years later than that of England, but was its natural offspring. Both of these trace back to the work of John Knox, and both left the world better. In contrast with such Revolutions came later that civil horror known as the French Revolution, which only wrought ruin because destitute of the spirit of true Reformation. It broke down the Inquisition, but put nothing good in its place. In 1906 disestablishment comes as a bloodless revolution.

As I write these pages, there breaks on the startled world the thunder of Revolution in the Russian Empire. It seems to presage the fulfillment of the teaching of Knox concerning the rights of man; nor can Turkey, China, or Persia escape. The dragon's power is broken in far Thibet, while the Crescent of the cruel Moslem fades out. Does it not signify a fulfillment of the Scripture, "The removing of those things that are shaken that those things that are not shaken may remain?"

CHAPTER III.

SCHOLARSHIP.

THE question has been raised whether Knox was
as great a scholar as Luther, Calvin, Melanchthon,
or Zwingli. The mere comparison is not very im-
portant, except as the question may bear upon the
equipment of our Reformer for his own work. It is
certain he could not have been the mighty preacher
he was whereby he did his chief reforming work
had he not been a man of high scholarship as well
as intellectual endowments. There is a style of
scholarship that might have divided his power and
detracted from his success. He was too great a
man for theological hairsplitting and trivial discus-
sion of linguistic roots or hermeneutical trifling.
Such men are useful, but very tiresome unless they
rise above it. In the higher sense of learning, he
reminds one of St. Paul, who certainly might have
been a very great and learned rabbi, or brilliant

scribe, or renowned orator, had he developed in either direction; but with his motto, "This one thing I do," he gave up any development in multiform ways or an exhibition of all-round scholarship.

As with most men of great usefulness, much of Knox's preparation for his career came unawares. While he was a pupil under John Major, acquiring the scholarship of the Renaissance, he was unwittingly imbibing Protestant ideas. That learning not only dealt in logic and literature, but sowed the seeds of democracy. This germinated into fruit as he confronted Mary, Queen of Scots, and took the position that if rulers became unrighteous, their people might call them to account. This his civics was in turn propagated in the civil government of Scotland, and later in the American colonies.

He was an earnest student of the Church Fathers, specially of Jerome and Augustine. He was also something of a linguist. His preaching, as well as his five volumes of history of the Scotch Reformation and his voluminous correspondence, shows that he uses the colloquial, mongrel English with great effect. A few samples of this may bring out the man and his times more definitely.

In his celebrated "First Blast of the Trumpet against the Monstrous Regiment of Women," he

5

says, "To promote a woman to bear rule, superiority, dominion, or empire, is a thing most contrarious
to His revealed well." From his "Historie:" "Sum
said Utheris hued the branches of papistry, bot he
straiketh at the rute to destroy the whole. Utheris
said gif the magistri nostri defend not now the pope
and his authoritie, which is impugnit, the devill have
my part of him and his lawes. Thairfoir we wald
counsail yow and thame to provyde better defenses
than fyre and sword." When Knox was yet a galley slave he wrote: "I mene not that any man in
extremitie of trubill can without dolour and without feer of trubill to follow. Trubill and feir are
the verie spurris to prayer."

"I the wryter hereof (lat it be said to the laude
and prais of God allone), in angusche of mynd and
vehement tribulatioun and afflictioun, called to the
Lord when not only the ungodlie but even my faithful brethren, ye and my awn self, judgeit my cause
to be irremedeable, and yit my greatest calamitie,
and when my panis wer most cruell wold His eternal wisdome that my handis suld wryt far contrarie
to the judgment of Carnall reasone, whilk His mer-
cie hath pruved trew. Blessit be His halie name."

This vigorous, idiomatic mongrel speech would
enable him to lead his countrymen far more effect-

ively than would the elegant English of Shakespeare or the present pure speech of Edinburgh.

It is a matter of regret to find the Scotch dialect fading out. The world is indebted to such as Sir Walter Scott, George Macdonald, Crockett, "Ian Maclaren," and Barrie for embalming this beautiful patois in fiction of a high order. There seems so much heartsomeness in words like "dour" for bold, "speer" for ask, "byre" for cow-house, "hemmel" for muley-cow, "ain" for own, "auld" for old, "bairns" for children, "blat" for bashful, "braes" for hillsides, "chiel" for stripling, "ding" for beat, "fash" for trouble, "ken" for know, "syne" for since, "lippen" for lean. "The broomy knowl over the Grannoch water."

He wrote "The History of the Reformation in Scotland" in five books, besides papers and letters, public and private, all marked by keen insight, wealth of thought, clearness of expression. Amid all his writings he published but one sermon.

He acquired other tongues. He would converse with Mary, Queen of Scots, in French, and preached in that language as fluently as in English. It was necessary for him, in order to be ordained as a Catholic priest, to understand Latin, the language used in their forms of worship. Greek was regarded with suspicion, but he acquired it before he was of middle age. His love of learning was all the more emphasized in taking up the study of Hebrew at his earliest opportunity when fifty years of age. While pastor of his congregation at Geneva, there was a cluster of scholars eminent enough to send forth the Geneva Bible, which became so popular and held on so well that it was carried in the pockets of Cromwell's soldiers eighty years later, and for a long time competed with King James's version, in the production of which it furnished great assistance. In this Knox was a helper and director. Measured by his literary monuments, he was scholar up to the needs of his task, the completest Reformation of the sixteenth century.

BLUNDERER.

Knox blundered, for he was human. In his "Trumpet Blast against the Regiment of Women," issued from Geneva, where he was in exile, he was premature and too sweeping. This he afterwards conceded, thus exhibiting a moral courage greater than had he refused to make the concession. In this he was like Luther, who hastily attempted to bridge the chasm from papal idolatry to freedom with his fiction of consubstantiation. Both remind one of the Apostle Paul, who conceded to the council his own mistake in rebuking the high priest, saying, "I wist not, brethren, that he was the high priest." Only an inspired prophet is warranted in being as personal as Knox while preaching.

Many a mistake has been made in quoting "Thou art the man." Plainness of speech when impertinent or insolent may do great harm; when kind and personal it may be as beneficial as sunlight. Nathan rebuked the King in private and won him over to repentance. In public he might have miserably failed. A John the Baptist may cry out "O generation of vipers." None but a prophet such as Nathan and the great Forerunner are sure of their charges. Gladstone was a great man, but when making his maiden speech in Parliament he defended his father in slave-holding; he began as a Tory in politics; he expressed sympathy with the Southern Confederacy in the day of our distress, but he was great enough to yield to conviction and recant in all three of these mistakes.

John Knox did apologize to Elizabeth. Judge from his own language to her whether he made amends for his "trumpet blast."

"Nothing in my book contained is or can be prejudicial to your Grace's just regiment, provided that you be not found ungrateful unto God. Ungrate you shall be proved in presence of His throne, howsoever the flatterers justify your acts, if you transfer the glory of that in which you now stand to any other thing than to the dispensation of His mercies, which only maketh that truthful to your Grace which nature and law denieth to all women. Neither would I that your Grace should fear that this your humiliation before God should, in any case, infirm and weaken your just and lawful authority before men. Nay, Madam, such unfeigned confession of God's benefits received shall be the establishment of the same, not only to yourself but also to your seed and posterity; where, contrariwise, a proud conceit and elevation of yourself shall be the occasion that your reign shall be unstable, troublesome and short. God is witness that unfeignedly I both reverence and love your Grace; yea, I pray that your reign may be long, prosperous, and quiet; and that for the quietness which Christ's members, before persecuted, have received under you. Yet, if I should flatter your Grace, I were no friend, but a deceitful traitor; and, therefore, of conscience I am compelled to say, that neither the consent of people, process of time, nor multitude of men can establish a law which God shall approve; but, whatsoever He approveth by His eternal Word that shall be approved, and whatsoever He damneth that shall be condemned, though all men on earth should hazard the justification of the same. And therefore, Madam, the only way to retain and keep these benefits of God, abundantly poured out of late days upon you and your realm, is unfeignedly to render unto God's mercy and undeserved grace the whole glory of this your exaltation. Forget your birth and all title which thereupon doth hang, and consider deeply how for fear of your life you did decline from God and bow in idolatry. Let it not appear a small offence in your eyes that you have declined from Christ Jesus in the day of His battle. Neither yet would I that you should esteem the mercy to be vulgar and common which you have received, to-wit, that God hath covered your former offences, hath preserved you when you were most unthankful, and in the end hath exalted and raised you up not only from the dust but also from the ports of death to rule over His people for the comfort of His Kirk. It appertaineth to you, therefore, to ground the justness of your authority not upon that law which from year to year doth change, but upon the eternal providence of Him who, contrary to nature and without your deserving, hath thus exalted your head. If thus in God's presence you humble yourself, as in my heart I glorify God for that rest granted to His afflicted flock within England under you, a weak instrument, so will I with my tongue and pen justify your authority and regiment as the Holy Ghost hath justified the same in Deborah, that blessed mother in Israel. But, if these premises (as God forbid) be neglected, and you shall begin to brag of your birth and build your authority upon your law, flatter you whoso list, your felicity shall be short. Interpret my words in the best part, as written by him who is no enemy to your Grace."

We also find him involved in a ruse. He encouraged Elizabeth to send troops to the aid of the Scotch, suggesting that England might send them and then escape reproach from France by disowning them as rebels. While not apologizing for this duplicity, how very slight and innocent it seems compared with the theory, "All things are fair in war!"

He further blundered by accepting the theory, prevalent in his day, uniting things civil and religious. It was the case with Rome, with France, with

Spain, with the English Episcopacy, and in this John Calvin at Geneva blundered with all the rest of them. It remains the embarrassment and bane of the English Establishment, and we yet hear echoes of a "National Church of America." This the Archbishop of Canterbury disowns.

We break away from the past reluctantly. Old habits, like unbroken cords, may be hard to discover and sever. Too wild a dash into the unknown may be perilous for the future while it forfeits the good already gained. The reforms of the sixteenth century did not entirely sever Church and State nor allow freedom of opinion. Sometimes the reformers seized upon the rod of their own oppressors and in turn used it to compel faith. Calvin approved of the execution of Servetus. Beza, the accomplished scholar, by an elaborate argument, full of honest fallacy, justified it. That argument in brief was "Heresy is disturbing to the Church and should be prevented. The civil power and not the ecclesiastical should see to it. Cæsar beareth not the sword in vain, therefore Servetus should have been executed." While Knox did not spoil his career by executing an opponent, he did not disapprove, but seemed to favor the conduct of Calvin in this. He would have applied this logic to Bothwell and Mary Queen of Scots, but fortunately could not. The same disability would have been a great good fortune to our Puritan ancestors in America.

The Savior of the world held up a beacon-light whereby all this folly might have been avoided. Jesus alone never made mistakes. It was He who said, "Who made me a judge or divider over you?" "My kingdom is not of this world;" "Render unto Cæsar the things that are Cæsar's, and unto God the things that are God's;" "Put up thy sword; they that take the sword shall perish by the sword."

Knox, with the rest of them, blundered in transferring the theocracy of the Old Testament into the polity of the Christian dispensation.

In spite of this mistake, we find his theory, as incorporated in the organization of the new government of Scotland in 1560, an adjustment out of which has come the American government with separation of Church and State. In that organization it was distinctly provided that the civil power should be secondary to the Kirk, and yet be required to support it. Here was unfortunately left a lingering tie of embarrassment, out of which came the

"Established Kirk of Scotland," and, on account of this lingering bond of union, most of the splits in that Kirk.

We Americans have not reached perfection in this separation of Church and State. We have rather gone beyond it. So nearly have we divorced the secular from the religious as to imperil both.

The Roman Catholic theory, if successful, would endanger our public schools and threaten our nation. Though the practice of the papal Church has changed, its theory has not. It should not be allowed to dominate and so destroy our system of popular education. That system, as we shall show, started from Knox. But, so far as the Bible has become a banished book, we go against its Author and His heir the child.

The recent attempts to restore it as literature and ethics show signs of sanity. In so far as Roman Catholics claim that education is character-building, and religion an essential element and the State incompetent for that, they are right. Protestant Americans relegate that to the Church and the home. This is also right, but does not go far enough.

To admit Minerva and Œdipus, Shakespeare and Horace, Darwin and Froebel, and expel Moses and

Jesus, is a revolt, which tends to Atheism in our schools.

The efforts to place the name of God in the Constitution would seem superfluous since He is there recognized. We have our chaplaincies in army, congress, and court-room. The government protects all people in their rights to worship God as conscience shall dictate. We are the freest people on earth and the best governed, but it remains to convert our art, commerce, politics, and social life back to where they each started at the beginning, bringing them again under the inspiration of religion.

It may indicate the growing necessity of this to note that time was, in this country, when the minister was the dominating man in community. Later on the teacher divided with him that ascendency. The editor came along, and captured another large segment of the clergymen's control. The one now in the saddle is the commercial man. This man, when he becomes a plutocrat, often invades the editorial realm, directing the policy of journalism. He enters the common school and the secular university to direct what they shall be.

In the denominational university he is apt to become dictator to the Board of Trustees, director as to who shall be president, and practically chooses the professors in the various departments, himself unacquainted with the genius and progress necessary to their truest work. He can, and sometimes does, become arbiter of the policy of the Church, deciding whether it shall have an adequate house of worship and when, greatly influencing the choice of ministry. There is danger that the civil government, the newspaper world, the university, and the Church will be found bowing down at the feet of the Dagon of wealth.

Hard after this man in the saddle rides the pursuer after amusement, pleasure, and indulgence. Here is a loud call for the Edwardses, the Finneys, the Moodys, and the hundred and forty thousand Christian ministers, with the millions of earnest people, whose life is consecrated to the doctrine of Him who commanded, "Seek first the kingdom of God." All the great elements of human society, art, literature, law, agriculture, and trade took their origin in religion, whether pagan, Jewish, or Christian. This excessive tendency in our country to divorce them must be reversed, and its accomplishment lies upon the Church. Knox was right in so far as he placed civil and secular affairs subordinate to religion. What they need is regeneration rather than subjugation.

WAS KNOX A HYPER-CALVINIST?

Here is a partial portrait of Calvin drawn by Dr. Philip Schaff:

"He kindled the religious fire which roused the moral and intellectual strength of Holland, and consumed the dungeons of the Inquisition and the fetters of the political despotism of Spain. His genius left a stronger mark on the national character of the Anglo-Saxon race and the Churches of Great Britain than their native Reformers. His theology and piety raised Scotland from a semi-barbarous condition, made it the classical soil of Presbyterian Christianity, and one of the most enlightened, energetic, and virtuous countries on the face of the globe. His spirit stirred up the Puritan Revolution of the seventeenth century, and his blood ran in the veins of Hampden and Cromwell as well as Baxter and Owen. He may be called, in some sense, the spiritual Father of New England and the American Republic."

Dr. Schaff was a Switzer; he pays a fine tribute, but, like some of the Swiss water-powers, tosses the spray wider than the channel and appropriates some of the work of Knox and other Reformers to Calvin.

Knox was Calvinist by conviction, personal attachment, and reverence for the man whose name has overshadowed the originator of this embarrassing scheme of religious metaphysics; not St. Augustine but John Calvin gives name to it. Knox, though older in years, began later in life, and learned much from the great Genevan besides Hebrew. He was assigned the task of defending Calvinism. Like many another creed, it has needed most defending at its weakest side.

Knox did it well, for he had gifts for such work. But, when run back to its higher sources nearer heaven, it practically meets in harmony with Arminian views. Neither robs any man of a chance for salvation, and compels no one. However inconsistent in logic, fatalism is denied by most Calvinists, whether in the Westminster Confession or not. So Arminians claim the entire helplessness of man to save himself, and each man doubts total depravity in his own babe, but champions the Divine sovereignty. Fatalism has its home mostly in modern fiction.

"IT DOTH NOT YET APPEAR."

No man's full potentialities are used in what he does. General Grant amazed the world by his latent power as a writer, after a military career scarcely equaled in history. John Wesley was competent to have eclipsed Wellington as a military commander, or Pitt as a statesman. St. Paul could have equaled Aristotle in logic, or Demosthenes in oratory. Knox could have been Socratic as a teacher, or a Demosthenes as orator, or a Cavour as statesman. He had not time for these, but must leave them for his gigantic progeny; to the mention of whom we shall recur later.

Lest I seem excessive in admiration, let me quote from others. Froude, who could show up his own England to her disadvantage when he saw occasion, and who showed a doubtful fidelity in the way he exposed the literary remains of Carlyle, who could whitewash Julius Cæsar into a plausible character, has thus expressed himself concerning Knox: "He was no narrow fanatic, who, in a world in which God's grace was equally visible in a thousand creeds, could see truth and goodness nowhere but in his own formula. He was a large, noble, generous man, with a shrewd perception of actual fact, who found himself face to face with a system of hideous iniquity. He believed himself a prophet, with a direct commission from heaven to overthrow it, and his return to Scotland became the signal, therefore, for the renewal of the struggle."

This stands sharply over against the passionate misjudgment of Hume, who showed his own inability to fairly weigh testimony by his celebrated absurdity, supposed to be an argument against miracles.

Froude further says: "He taught the peasant of the Lothians that he was a free man, the equal in the sight of God with the proudest peer or prelate that had trampled on his forefathers. He was the one antagonist whom Mary Stewart could not soften nor Maitland deceive. He it was that raised the poor commoners of his country into a stern and rugged people. The time has come when English history may do justice to one but for whom the Reformation would have been overthrown among ourselves; for the spirit which Knox created saved Scotland, and if Scotland had been Catholic again, Elizabeth's ministers, nor the teaching of her bishops, nor Elizabeth's chicaneries would have preserved England from revolution. But for him, Mary Stewart would have bent Scotland to her purpose, and Scotland would have been the lever which France and Spain would have worked on

6

England.   Elizabeth would have been flung off her throne, or have gone back into the Egypt to which she was too often casting wistful eyes."

Carlyle, in his essay on Sir Walter Scott, speaks of Knox on this wise: "Honor to all the brave and true, everlasting honor to brave old Knox, one of the truest of the true! That in the moment while he and his cause, amid civil broils in convulsion and confusion, were still but struggling for life, he sent the schoolmaster forth into all corners, and said, 'Let the people be taught,'—this is but one, and indeed an inevitable and incomparatively inconsiderable item in his great message to men. His message in its true compass was, 'Let men know that they are men, created by God, responsible to God, who work in any meanest moment of time what will last to eternity,'—this great message Knox did deliver with a man's voice and strength, and found a people to believe him. The Scotch national character originates in many circumstances; first of all, in the Saxon stuff there was to work on, but next, and beyond all else except that, in the Presbyterian gospel of John Knox."

In his "Heroes and Hero Worship" he speaks thus: "This that Knox did for his nation we may really call a resurrection as from death. It was not a smooth business, but it was welcome surely, and cheap at that price had it been far rougher. The people began to live. Scotch literature and thought, Scotch industry, James Watt, David Hume, Walter Scott, Robert Burns,—I find Knox and the reformation acting in the heart's core of every one of these persons. It seems to me hard measure that this Scottish man, after three hundred years, should have to plead like a culprit before the world; intrinsically for having been in such a way as it was then possible to be, the greatest of all Scotchmen. Had he been a poor half-and-half, he could have crouched into the corner like so many others; Scotland had not been delivered, and Knox had been without blame. He bared his breast to battle, had to row in French galleys, wander forlorn in exile, in clouds and storms; was censured, shot at through his windows; had a right sore fighting life. If this world were his place of recompense, he had made but a bad venture of it. I can not apologize for Knox. For one I will remark that this post of prophet to his nation was not of his seeking.

"Knox's conduct to Queen Mary, the harsh visits he used to make in her own palace to reprove her there have been much commented on. On reading the actual narrative of what Knox said and what

he meant, I must say one's tragic feeling is rather
disappointed.   They are not so coarse, these
speeches; they seem to me about as fine as the circumstances would permit.   Knox was not there to
act as courtier.   He came on another errand.   Knox
was the constitutional opposition party in Scotland;
the nobles of the country, called by their station to
take that post, were not found in it.   Knox had to
go or no one.   Withal unexpectedly enough, this
Knox has a vein of drollery.   He has a true eye for
the ridiculous.   His history, with its rough earnestness, is curiously enlivened with this.   A true, loving, illuminating laugh mounts up over the earnest
visions; not a loud laugh you would say, a laugh in
the eyes most of all.   They go far wrong who think
this Knox was a gloomy, spasmodic, shrieking
fanatic.   Not at all.   He is one of the solidest of
men, practical, cautious, hopeful, patient.   A most
shrewd, observing, quietly discerning man; in fact,
he has very much the type of character they assign
to the Scotch at present.   A sore fight, but he won
it. 'Have you hope?' he was asked in his last moment when he could no longer speak.   He lifted his
finger, pointed upwards, and so died.   Honor to
him.   His works have not died."

The Scotchman is highly endowed.   Among his

gifts is his susceptibility to superstition. While this quality may lead to darkness and disaster, without it the soul were shorn of its wings and rendered incapable of art, poetry, and religion. It is doubtful whether the Wesley family could have produced its great hymn writer and his brother, the great religious leader, had they been destitute of that quality which haunted the Epworth rectory with ghosts.

The German with his spooks and "man of the Hartz Mountains" makes pietism possible and opens the door for the Moravian and German Methodism, the chief hope of emancipation from rationalism and beer.

The quality which peopled the "Heilands" with "bogies" and the meddlesome "diel" which holds on through Sir Walter's stories and yet pervades the American descendants, these qualities made possible the orators, poets, writers of romance, leaders in philosophy and missionary heroes, yet leading mankind.

REFORM AND REVIVAL.

The sixteenth century and the twentieth century may mutually illustrate each other. There are yet New Englanders who call a revival a "Reforma-

tion," and they are right. A revival without reformation, and a Reformation without a revival, both
breed death. "Faith without works is dead." Which
should precede the other were hard to tell. They
are inseparable. One leads legitimately to the
other. Did Knox emphasize reform excessively to
the neglect of the revival? The opportunity opened
by him for the Wesleyan movement near two hundred years later was improved so as to effect much
reform, but was chiefly the most gracious revival
after Pentecost to that time.

In 1858 a remarkable revival spread all over
America and swept across the world to London, and
thence to Edinburgh and Glasgow and Aberdeen,
returning something of Knox's seed-sowing in a
rich harvest. Later on, in the year 1873, Moody
and Sankey, under a Divine impulse, invaded Scotland with a revival, which brought the learning of
the foremost universities of the English-speaking
world to unite with the unlettered Moody in bowing at the feet of Jesus. It was a fair spectacle before angels and men, when these seats of metaphysics, philosophy, and most enlightened Biblical
criticism came in childlike simplicity to the cross
of Christ with the lay preacher. They in turn now

lead the learned world in clustering nearer to Christ.

There has been a lull and a time of waiting for the outbreak of the next great revival. For a decade there have been men on the outlook throughout Christendom, and that means as never before in the round world. These watchmen have seemed to catch notes as of the sound of a mighty wind from heaven. There have also been cautions against prophesying a great awakening, lest we presume to know in advance the mind of God, but this expectation has steadily increased and spread abroad.

In 1903, in India, Bishop Thoburn baptized in one week 1,747 people, and has repeatedly declared that ten millions more are possible within ten years. These raw heathen are transformed into witnessing martyrs, both in spirit and in practice.

Wales has surpassed the days of Griffith Jones, Howell Harris, and Whitefield, with a revival that has moved men of all grades, from the strongest characters down to the workers in the pits. The beasts of burden could not understand their converted drivers because of the absence of former profanity.

The sturdy Presbyterian Church anticipated the

aggressive Methodist denomination in a nation-wide, organized, irresistible, and contagious revival movement.

The Methodist Episcopal Church, with the most thorough organization of any, except the Roman Catholic, has resolved to utilize her machinery, but not to depend upon it. There is a rapidly growing "World League of Prayer." She is evidently drawing near the spirit of him who said, "I will not let thee go," and also close to the heart of Him who seems to say, "Can you not discern signs and times?"

Ere this is in print the greatest revival of all the past will be here, or again Jesus will have cause to cry, "O that thou hadst known in this day the things that belong unto peace! but now they are hid from thine eyes!"

PART III.

MONUMENTS.

CHAPTER I.

HIS MONUMENTS.

WHERE are they? Those of marble and brass are ever comparatively insignificant. At the American Capital is a very lofty pillar to the memory of Washington, five hundred and fifty-five feet high; but there is far more eloquence in the modest tomb at Mt. Vernon.

Where are those of Emerson, Hawthorne, Alcott, Thoreau, modest little headstones at Concord? Their thoughts are as prolific as the grapes from the old mother vine hard by. The brewer, however, saw to it while yet alive that marble splendor in that same cemetery should screen his name from the infamy and the sorrows produced by the beer mug. Where sleep Holmes, Longfellow, 'and Lowell? It is hard to find their monuments in Mount Auburn, but the *Atlantic Monthly,* founded by them, is only one of the shafts keeping their memory green.

Go to Geneva; the lofty equestrian statue of the

Duke of Brunswick mounts high above the city of the dead. By the mouth of the Rhone you will find the Island of Rousseau and a statue in bronze of the "wild, self-torturing sophist;" but find the tomb of John Calvin if you can.

Go to London, and you may find Sir David Wilkie's picture of Knox in his pulpit, preaching to his Edinburgh congregation. But we look in vain for any memorial of him in Westminster Abbey, that mausoleum of England's greatness. In Glasgow is a modest pillar to his memory.

Go to Edinburgh, and you can not avoid seeing the great and beautiful monument of Sir Walter Scott. It could scarcely be too fine for his transcendent genius. I am literary heretic enough to say that, if Shakespeare or Sir Walter must be spared, leave me the Scotch Wizard.

There is a modest statue of Knox preaching, also a stone-marker of the supposed burial place of John Knox behind the wall by St. Giles's Church. On the flat tablet is the simple inscription,

I K

1572

How appropriate the lines:

> "Let the sound of those he wrought for,
> Let the feet of those he fought for,
> Echo round his bones for evermore."

There is his house in Edinburgh, a queer old building which he occupied. It came so near falling down and so obstructed the street that the city authorities were about to remove it. The memory of Knox was too strong for the tide of time and modern life. Those who revered his memory rallied to preserve and renew the old house as near as possible after its former plans. Into this has been gathered a large number of relics, while mottoes taken from the sayings of Knox as well as others commemorate much of his life and the history of the Reformation.

But there is one relic not included among those collected there. That one escaped to America, down the line of his posterity, and is in possession of a lineal descendant somewhere in the State of Pennsylvania. It is an old clock, once the property of Knox. There is a Presbyterian Academy in South Salem, Ohio. One of the first two girl students to enter that school was named Susan Knox Stinson, a direct descendant from John Knox. If that old clock yonder, possibly at Lancaster, Pennsylvania, were still running, it would have ticked out the life of John Knox and Susan Knox Stinson; for both have gone.

The Stone of Scone Suggests Him.

For a long time it was at Iona, one of the Hebrides, on the west coast of Scotland. This island was the home of a pure Christianity according to the Gospel. The teachers and preachers were called Culdees. It was not a monastery, but a seminary. It survived amid monastic tyranny and licentiousness for centuries. It was the morning star of the day of Knox, which came on eight hundred years later. That stone was used as the coronation seat until, about 1296, Edward I, after a battle, carried it to London. It now rests beneath the coronation chair in Westminster Abbey. It remained a captive of war for over four centuries.

Now it symbolizes the mighty support of the British throne furnished by the rugged Scottish nation. Were it a diamond, brilliant as the Koh-i-noor, it could not vie in worth with that character which it symbolizes. That character had not been but for Knox. The stone is therefore his memorial.

"Hold Fast Our Confession."

One of the tallest, most comprehensive monuments is the Confession of Faith, which he, more than any other man, provided for the Convention of 1560, and out of which afterwards sprang a succession of confessions and covenants down to one hundred years later, the Westminster Confession and Catechism, around which Presbyterianism throughout the world still gathers, and, though it is slowly hewn away in some of its sharper angles, promises to abide as a magnificent expression of catholic Christianity for ages yet to come.

This is one of the monuments of John Knox, looming far above all symbols of marble or bronze.

This may be as favorable a time as any to call attention to some of the essentials of catholic unity between other great religious denominations and Presbyterians. Why should Baptist, Congregational, Lutheran, or Methodist antagonize the Presbyterian as though he were a heretic? That folly was rebuked long ago by Paul when the Corinthians were saying, "I am of Paul, I am of Apollos, I of Cephas, and I of Christ."

Knox made Brown and Congregationalism possible; he set the pace for John Bunyan with his "Pilgrim" written in jail, and Roger Williams, a Pilgrim to Rhode Island under compulsion, and hence the Baptist Church in the United States. But for Knox, the dissenting iconoclast, it is doubtful whether John Wesley would have found his way so readily, one hundred and seventy-nine years later, into the greatest revival up to that time.

Distinctness of view is helped by comparing, especially when we can so strike the merits as to see with more clearness and charity the differences and mutual defects. Thus we learn from others how to improve ourselves and how to avoid conformity in outward modes that degenerate, and seize upon matters that are vital in other than our own denomination.

With this purpose let us compare two of the mightiest Christian Protestant religions on earth, the followers of Knox and of Wesley. One launched in Edinburgh in 1560, the other in London one hundred and seventy-nine years after; the one purposely opposed to prelacy, the other so in spite of itself. Both are Presbyterial, believing that Episcopos and Presbuteros are identical so far as they signify ecclesiastical rank. Both are opposed to the union of Church and State. The Scotch Presbyterians were slow in attaining this liberty, while Methodism was never recognized by the State in England. In this country both were born free. As to doctrine, the Presbyterians are Calvinists, but in practice deny the fatalism of that system. The Methodists are Arminians, but in a greatly modified form, so as to avoid its Antinomian features and acknowledge the Divine sovereignty. Presbyterians believe in the "assurance of faith." Methodists emphasize the "witness of the Spirit." Both believe in total depravity and the sinner's inability to convert himself. Both are advancing in their earnest appeals to men on the basis of free will, power to repent, believe, and be saved. Both are growing powers in the world. Their appeal to Scripture is striking, as seen in the language of both Johns, Presbyterian and Methodist. "If any man shall note, in this our Confession, any article or sentence repugnant to God's Holy Word, may it please him of his gentleness and for charity's sake to admonish us, and we do promise satisfaction from the mouth of God, or reformation of that which he shall prove to be amiss." (Knox in the Confession.)

"The Holy Scripture contains all things necessary to salvation; so that whatsoever is not read therein, nor may be proved thereby, is not to be required of any man that it should be required as an article of faith." (Article of Faith incorporated from the Church of England by John Wesley into the Methodist Discipline.)

The Presbyterians have always insisted on a highly educated ministry, and have even crippled their power by the exclusive application of school requirements at the door of entry into the ministry. Methodism, born in Oxford University, has never as a denomination favored illiteracy, but has seized upon available material for immediate necessities, and so outrun Presbyterianism in both city and country.

In pushing forward the founding of institutions of learning the "Log College," now Princeton University, is followed in America with fifty-five others, while in Scotland all the world may bow to Glasgow, Aberdeen, and Edinburgh. The wish of Knox that the Kirk might "be preserved from the bondage of the universities" has been fulfilled.

Methodism, with lavish hand, scattered the seeds of university life across America from ocean to ocean, until there are 225 of all grades in spite of multitudes of abortive plants which should have died. These have been wisely co-ordinated in a high standard of admission and graduation, until the founding of the American university at the Capital of the country promises to stimulate the whole system. Nor has the Wesleyan Methodism of England neglected to establish institutions of learning of very high grade.

In form of government these two great Churches are nearly identical. The Presbyterian has in local Churches the session; the Methodist has the Official Board. The Presbytery in the one is answered by the Quarterly Conference in Methodism. The Presbyterian Synod, a combination of equal lay and clerical members, is answered in Methodism by the Annual Conference, exclusively clerical, except as influenced by a powerful non-membership laity.

The highest governing body of Presbyterianism is the General Assembly, equally lay and clerical. The Methodists are governed by the General Conference, also equally divided between laymen and clergymen.

The presiding officer of the highest Presbyterial body is elective from time to time, and called "moderator." The Methodist bishops are no more than moderators, presiding in turn without power of speech or vote, and amenable to the General Conference for fidelity in the administration of office.

A striking difference between the two is in the mode of supervising the pastoral relation. Theoretically, and in large measure practically, Methodist pastors are appointed to their work by a bishop, assisted by a council of presiding elders. These presiding elders, appointed by the bishop, each has supervision of the pastors within his district, during the Conference year. He may not be presiding elder longer than six years at a time, while at present there is no time limit to the pastorate. This presiding eldership provides as far as practicable that there shall be no congregation left without ministerial supply. The District Conference of Methodism, composed of laymen and clergymen, has no parallel in the sister Church.

The founder of Methodism said, "I seek an alliance, offensive and defensive, with all who love our Lord Jesus Christ." Tardily at first, but now with increasing warmth, the Presbyterian Church is accepting the alliance.

On the question of episcopacy there has been much ado about nothing. A Methodist Presiding Elder is a Bishop; a Methodist General Superintendent is also a Bishop; a Presbyter is a Bishop; none of them belong to a separate order. Prelacy is a fiction and injurious only when lording it over God's heritage. John Knox prepared a book of Discipline. In it were these provisions: The difficulties created by the greatness of the field and the paucity of the laborers required two extra offices, neither of which has maintained its place in the Presbyterian system.

The first was that of readers, who are to read prayers and the Scriptures but were unable to exhort. They were encouraged to attempt a few words of exhortation and instruction and if these efforts succeeded, they might look forward to promotion to the superior office. The other was that of superintendents. Areas were allotted to them severally. Not unlike to the sees of bishops within which they were to erect the fabric of the Reformed Church. They were not only to plant new charges but to examine the life, diligence, and behavior of ministers, and also the order of their Churches and the manners of the people. "Provision must be made not only for the sustentation of the ministers themselves during their lives, but also for their wives and children after them, for we consider it a thing most contrarious to reason, godliness, and equity that the widow and children of him who in his life did faithfully serve the kirk of God and for that cause did not carefully make provision for his family, should, after his death, be left comfortless of all provision." An ideal to be better followed in our day. The Church may be shamed by the railways and the State in providing for retired employees. In this, at least, Carnegie is a follower of Knox.

We have not lost sight of the monuments of Knox in this comparison.

Coming back to covenants three years before that of 1560, when Scotland was really born as a nation, there had been a partial movement toward the same end, and this habit of entering into covenants and confessions of faith swept on down through three hundred years.

Charles I undertook to foist prelacy on Scotland sixty-five years after the death of Knox. As an outcome of this, Charles lost his head twelve years afterwards. A better head than Puritans are apt to concede. It may be as well to give here some account of how it happened. At the time (1637) Laud was the archbishop. Inspired by Charles in his movements, he appeared in St. Giles Cathedral Church in Edinburgh with pompous regalia. Jennie Geddes, whose identity has been challenged by some trivial criticisms, was seated on a stool in the audience. As the archbishop proceeded with the collects, she mistook the word for "colic" and shouted, "Villain, dost thou say mass at my lug?" and seizing her stool, hurled it at Laud. The people took up the cry against popery, and the riot extended through the country into a revolution, defeating Charles's purpose. He had intended to impose prelacy first on Scotland, and afterward on the American Colonies, so that the club which was broken by the stool of Jennie Geddes never fell upon the head of young America.

What great things from small beginnings! A boy threw a stone at a priest in Perth, and the cathedrals and monasteries were stripped of their works of art. Peter the Great spoke a word, and millions of serfs were emancipated. The bell rang out of the tower of Old South Church in Boston, and Paul Revere mounted and rode. His successors still ride on. At Lexington they "fired the shot heard round the world." April 12, 1861, a man touched the fuse to fire on Fort Sumter. That knocked the shackles from three million slaves, as well as the coming millions of whites. A rioter flung an epithet at a Russian officer in the palace yard at St. Petersburg, Sunday, January 22, 1905, and a collision followed, shaking the empire. So the stool of Jennie Geddes, keeper of a vegetable store, knocked the club from the hand of tyranny, aimed at posterity. For all these great results from apparently small causes, the conditions were ripe. It needed but the match to set the world on fire.

The Scotch were a covenanting people. Let the world look out for such.

The year following the Revolution started by that stool, the National Covenant was renewed at Gray Friars, Edinburgh. Sixty thousand people came from all parts of Scotland, filling the Church and even the graveyard. They listened solemnly to the reading of the Covenant. Then, with trembling hand, the Earl of Sutherland first signed the parchment roll; then a stream of people came signing amid weeping and shouting, "some adding to their names, "Till death;" others drew blood from their own veins with which to write their names, till at last there was but room for initials, and the parchment was entirely covered. This was sixty-six years after the death of Knox. Covenanting is well as far as it goes, but all human history shows that it is easy to forget. In five years after the National Covenant came another, called "The Solemn League and Covenant." This was to cover the three kingdoms, England, Ireland, and Scotland; but it was vitiated by the mixture of civil and religious elements. It was, however, entered upon with intense enthusiasm by all three of the kingdoms. It

was destined to short life, and was finally burned
eighteen years afterwards by the hangman in Westminster Abbey.

The Westminster Confession.

This came also in the time of Charles I. The
Assembly was called against the wishes of the king
by the Long Parliament. It was composed of English and Scotch. Three Americans—John Cotton,
Thomas Hooker, and John Davenport—were invited,
but could not attend. The Churches were represented by Episcopalians, twelve Independents, some
Erastians, and some Presbyterians—in all one hundred and twenty-one men. Unitedly the Assembly
was composed of men of talent and learning unsurpassed in their time. The Independents and the
scholarly Erastians withdrew before the end of the
Assembly, while the Presbyterians continually increased, and became the controlling power. Their
work was deliberately done, requiring five and a
half years and 1,163 sessions before it went forth
from that Jerusalem chamber. There was much
fasting and prayer; some of the prayers were even
two hours long. No wonder the Confession en-
dures. The Assembly came under the Long Parliament. Both passed away together, but left the great

Confession an abiding shaft to the memory of Knox.
He wrote that of 1560, its forerunner, in four days.

THE KIRK A MONUMENT.

In pointing out the creeds and covenants, have
we gotten away from Knox?   That were impossi-
ble, just as it would be to get away from Ben Nevis
until we could escape the waters flowing from his
sides into the Sound of Mull or Moray Forth, or
just as Mount Shasta follows one all the way of the
Sacramento through the Golden Gate.

In addition to the covenants was the Scottish
Kirk.

Emerson visited Carlyle in Scotland.   Standing
on a hill, Carlyle pointed to a church-spire in the
valley, and said: "Eighteen hundred years ago
Christ died on the cross in Palestine.   That built the
church in the valley yonder.   That brought you
and me together from the ends of the earth.   See
how all things work together."

Coming down only fifteen centuries from the
crucifixion, we may add, had not Knox protested
and stood through stress and storm, neither church-
spire, nor Carlyle and Emerson, nor reader or
writer, would have enjoyed our religious liberty.

The Schoolhouse.

John Knox outlined a system of general education open for all children, coupled with university privileges. This was in 1560. There was a special act passed promoting the same great enterprise in 1695. That movement toward popular education was not received with favor in England. It has taken all the time till now for the mother country to become thoroughly aroused to the necessity of an educated peasantry.

Governor Berkeley, of the Virginia Colony, about 1650, reported that there was no common school in existence in Virginia, and he hoped there would not be for the next hundred years. His lordship belonged to the Cavaliers, and reflected their distrust of education for the common people. They believed

> "A little learning is a dangerous thing,—
> Drink deep, or taste not the Pierian spring."

Knox's ideal reached America during her Colonial period. It found prolific soil until to-day there is "a church in every valley and a schoolhouse on every hillside." Thirty millions of worshipers, the very salt of the earth, pass in and out of these church doors, while about eighteen millions of school pupils pass in and out of the "little red school" under the American flag. The entire population of Spain is but ten millions, a little over half the number of our school-children, while that of Scotland is about five millions, or not one-third of these intellectual heirs of John Knox. Face the church or the schoolhouse in either case, take off your hat and bow reverently to the memory of Knox.

CHAPTER II.

BONNIE SCOTLAND.

THIS is one of the monuments of Knox, with a dark seam or two in its pure marble. It is with no pleasure we point them out, nor with invidious comparison, forgetful of similar as well as other shadowy lines attaching to all English-speaking nations. There was looseness in the marital relations of the ancient Scottish clansmen; this did not pass away in the later times of priest, abbot, and noble. It was shockingly prominent in court life during our Reformer's era; even to this day the ratio of illegitimates is so almost unbelievable that we abstain from statistics. May the pure spirit of Knox soon prevail so as no longer to entail such sorrow upon innocent children, not to speak of the horrors in the life of those sinning! The Reformer deemed adultery worthy of death.

There is also what is known as Scotch whisky. Would that the name might be cut in twain, robbing

it of the honored name of "Scotch!" There are in
our country flaming placards advertising cigars and
drinks that are insulting to the memory of such
men as Henry George and President Garfield. One
would imagine their bones to stir in their graves
could they read the advertisements beneath their
pictures on the face of our city walls. Why must
death-bed scenes of illustrious statesmen, Presidents,
and governors be made offensive with descriptions
of the death-dealing cigar? Scotch whisky still
poisons the noble blood of Scotland. Lately a fire
destroyed a storage of seven hundred thousand gal-
lons in Aberdeen, which released, broke away down
the streets of the city into the river Dee, and on like
a river of fire to the German Ocean. Let Carlyle
boast of Knox as a "cheery, social man, having his
pipe of Bordeaux in that old Edinburgh house of
his." Had Knox been alive to look on that fire
rolling down the streets of Aberdeen, doubtless his
serious face would have lighted up with gladness.
Our grandsires called "old rye" God's good creature,
and served it to their ministers; nor has the habit
fled entirely from among English preachers, who
tone up for the pulpit with this devil's stimulus
called by John Wesley "liquid fire and distilled
damnation." With hundreds of thousands of men

of Knox's fiber the liquor curse will pass out of our nation, soon to be followed, let us hope, by its twin curse, nicotine poison.

Over against these reluctant impeachments, I quote Dr. Philip Schaff: "Scotland is an unconquerable fort of orthodox Protestantism. In no other country and Church do we find such fidelity and tenacity; such unswerving devotion to the genius of the Reformation; such union of metaphysical subtlety with religious fervor and impetuosity; such general interest in ecclesiastical councils and enterprises; such jealousy for the rights and the self-government of the Church; such loyalty to a particular denomination, combined with a generous interest in Christ's kingdom at large; such reverence for God's Holy Word and holy day that, after the hard and honest toil of the week, lights up the poorest man's cottage on Saturday night."

Lofty tribute from a native Switzer to sons of Scotia; but both are mountain lands, famous for Protestant heroes.

Other Monuments.

Scotland has a large number of fine cities. We mention a few with over a hundred thousand population. Edinburgh, the capital, overhung with a

cloud of historic interest and decorated with very
fine modern architecture, wears as her brightest
jewel the famous university. It occupies the ground
of the "Kirk o' Field" and the murder of Darnley;
a nobler substitute than the obelisk of Luxor on the
blood spot of the guillotine in Paris.

Another great monument is Dundee, astride the
Tay, eight miles from the German Ocean, wonderful for its docks, its jute, its Baltic commerce, and
its trade with Canada and India. It has a cathedral
about old St. Mary's Tower and a university of
renown.

Further north is Aberdeen, by the Dee, and fac-
ing the German Ocean with its mighty pier, its
granite bridge, its woollens and Marischal College.

There is, on both banks of the Clyde, Glasgow.
next London in population, greatest in Scotland in
variety of manufactures and shipments. It has a
Gothic cathedral of great beauty, but its university
rises greater than all, the Alma Mater of Knox.

THE SCOTCH SABBATH AS A MONUMENT.

Scotchmen excel us. Knox set the pace. The
Pharisees overdid the benign law of the Sabbath,
so did they the law of the tithe, fasting, and prayer.
It is easy to make a yoke. There is much foolish

sneering at the Puritan Sunday among us, promoted mostly by men who despise all law, excepting greed and appetite. When Carl Schurz, as a fugitive, landed in Edinburgh, he sought an interview with a man of large business interests and was astonished to find that no business houses were open on the Lord's Day. His description of his experiences that day are comically eloquent, when one remembers the beer-garden habit of his native Germany. In our capital at Washington all government buildings are closed on the Sabbath-day, except the Library, and it were better for that to be closed. Go to Edinburgh and you will find that the divine law, "Remember the Sabbath-day to keep it holy," was no mistake on the part of the Almighty.

ROLL-CALL.

Omitting for the present any analysis of callings, let us run the eye down the alphabet and find the descendants of John Knox, who but for his work could not have been.

A. There were the Abercrombies, about the middle of the eighteenth century, very eminent in military service, literature, and science, both medical and moral.

B. Far back in the centuries, amid the shadows,

8

were the Bruces, mighty chieftains, celebrated in song and fiction. Of them came, after the Reformer, singers and explorers, also Barbour, poet, contemporary of Chaucer. There was Bell, who though born in Edinburgh, rang out the telephone from Boston; and Black, writer of romance; and Blackie, masterful molder of mind; and Blair, founder of William and Mary College, Virginia; and Browns to furnish martyr, physician, metaphysician, and to leave us "Rab and His Friends." And there were the Balfours, and Lord Brougham, a marvel of oratory and statecraft down to his ninetieth year; and George Buchanan of classic learning, writing poems in Latin; and one of the few hymn-writers of high order in our day, the late Horatius Bonar. The blood of Browning was tinged on the maternal side with Scotch. Sir Campbell-Bannerman, English premier, comes of the stock.

C. The Campbells were a gifted race, furnishing such a poet as could give the world "Lord Ullin's Daughter" and "Hohenlinden." How can we praise Chalmers, Carlyle, Calderwood, Carnegie, divines, orators, metaphysicians, and benefactors?

D. Come we to Douglas, family that furnished eight leaders slain in battle by the middle of the fifteenth century, and before Knox's time. "They that take the sword shall perish by the sword." But the name Douglas lives honored by lovers of peace. William Drummond was a rival of Ben Jonson. Dunbar was a courtly singer. Dalrymples, four of them, are noted for statecraft, law, war, and history.

E. The name of Erskine suggests a constellation in law, jurisprudence, and religion, who made the latter part of Scotland's eighteenth century brilliant.

F. Name Forbes, and you suggest high literary talent.

G. Grant means arts and sciences as well as military ability; one strand of which ended at Mount McGregor when our Ulysses died. Gladstone, peerless in his day, was of Scotch ancestry.

H. The Hamiltons were borderers, swinging to either side as best suited them through the long years of strife, but furnishing further down, the great, if not the greatest, metaphysician of his race, Sir William Hamilton. And there is Hogg, whose poetry deserves a better name. Hood breaks the heart with his "Song of the Shirt."

I. Irving was a brilliant, troublesome, fanatical, religious leader.

J. James, for the most part, but a titular name. There were six of them in a line; five of whom lost life in battle or by assassination. The fifth died of a broken heart on account of failure in battle; this was the father of Mary, Queen of Scots.

K. We come to the Keiths, gifted, martial, scholarly; one of them was the confidant of Frederick the Great, and died on the field of Hohenkirch. Another gave Marischal College and University to Scotland.

L. Sir David Lindsay, first of Scotch laureates; and Leyden, cosmopolitan, scholar, and traveler. The Leightons were an able and genial family. There were four Leslies, two great generals, one a diplomatist, one a physicist. Lockhart gave the *Edinburgh Quarterly Review* to the world as well as the "Life of Sir Walter Scott." When we say Livingstone, there emerges Africa and the sources of the Nile.

M. Many are the Macs. Macgregor, the "Rob Roy" of Sir Walter; George Macdonald, who threw floods of sunshine over Scottish hills and life; and Hector Archibald Macdonald, of Egypt, India, then South Africa, Major-General of Highlanders. The Montgomeries, three of them poets. The Moores, one physician and writer; and Sir John, whom we remember "with his martial cloak around him, left alone in his glory;" and the Morays, too distinguished to describe; the Muirs, one a Sanscrit scholar and one Arabic. John Muir, fosterer of our national parks, and whose monument is the Muir Glacier.

M. Murchison was the dominant geologist in his time. And there was Murdock who improved the steam-engine of Watt, and in 1792 produced illuminating gas and coal. And there is McAuley and McCosh lent to us for Princeton, and the Mackenzies and the McPhersons. The name of Hugh Miller suggests "Old Red Sandstone." To name McCrie is to mention the most thorough biographer, as well as the fairest, of Knox and Melville, and Matheson, whose physical blindness enhanced his spiritual vision, and McLaren, for fifty years preacher and expositor, growing richer each year.

N. Napier was the inventor of logarithms. The Nasmyths, father and son, were painters; while Patrick Nasmyth gave the steam-hammer to the world. Nichols, father and son, are noted in astronomy and literature. Nicol was the painter of "Irish Life;" Lady Nairne, "Imitator of Burns."

O. Mrs. Oliphant was a prolific novelist, at first a bit lonesome in Scotch leadership, being a woman. But her kind has come to the front. Drop the alphabet and group the women. Fanny Wright became our first woman lecturer. Three great lady travelers, Miss North, Darwinized, melancholy, widely traveled, a gifted artist; Mrs. Ella Bird Bishop, the conquerless cripple, wit, and orator, traveling amid the Asiatic nations, opening the way for the support of mission work an honor to Bonnie Scotland; Miss Constance E. Gordon Cumming, a descendant of Red Comyn, the touch of her wealth and genius diffusing itself over Christian Europe and unchristian China, where by her support Hill Murray teaches the blind to read and open their eyes on two worlds.

P. Playfair was philosopher and mathematician; Pinkerton, antiquarian and litterateur. Paterson rose from the rank of peddler to become the founder of the London Bank; he was so far-sighted as to be promoter of the first Panama or Darien enterprise in the seventeenth century; the colony thus founded was called New Caledonia; it was wrecked, as was that of the French near two centuries later. This Paterson also was a leader in the Union of Scotland and England, which succeeded better than the Darien enterprise. Pollok is immortal as the author of "The Course of Time."

R. Alexander Ross is famed as the author of "The Fortunate Shepherdess." There were four Ramsays, each brilliant; one started a circulating library, one was a geologist, one a chevalier, another a clergyman and writer. Reid, a great philosopher, who by his philosophy of common sense, offset the folly of Hume and Berkeley. He was followed by Stewart, Sir William Hamilton, and in our day by Calderwood. The Rennies, three of them, left their monuments, one at Sebastopol, one in London Bridge, and one at London Docks. To mention Roberts and Robertson is to suggest painting, military craft, antiquarian research, and history.

S. John Skinner, of "Tullochgorum." To name Scott is to speak of the painter, the philosopher, and Sir Walter. There were Shairp and Sharp, like their own names. Out of the great throngs of Smiths we need mention but two, Adam the political economist, and Robertson Smith, the Biblical scholar. Stephenson calls to mind a great engineer and the pathetic Robert Louis, with his "Jekyll and Hyde." To name the Stewarts suggests Sir Donald, military hero, and Dugald, the philosopher. Sterling stands for medicine and literature; Syme, the great surgeon; and Alexander Selkirk, who set the boy world in pursuit of Robinson Crusoe.

T. There were the Taits, one Archbishop of Canterbury, the other physicist and mathematician. Tannahill and Tennant. Thomas Telford was a great civil engineer. There were seven Thomsons, a naturalist, two poets, one painter, an explorer, a chemist, and an antiquary. Tyler left the bar for literature.

W. Sir William Wallace is traced so far back in the shadows of history as to appear somewhat dim, though there is a monumental tower more than two hundred feet high at Abbey Craig, establishing him firmly in Scottish history, for it is a sort of Valhalla for Scotland. Sir David Wilkie, a great painter with a poetic soul; it was he who gave the world the painting of "John Knox Preaching Before His Congregation in Edinburgh," now in the British Museum. To say Wilson is to name the distinguished archæologist, and "Sir Christopher North," and another great linguist missionary; and Wilson, who fell heir to the sword of Cameron when his hands were cut off. George Wishart, who led Knox into the light, was burned at St. Andrews.

Y. James Young, chemist, early in the nineteenth century, whose experiments led to the petroleum industry. Colonel Sir Henry Yule, a distinguished soldier in India, and an author of literary skill equal to his military talent. Possibly the letter Z is too angular to be at home in Scotland, unless softened to S, where it sits on the Shetland Isles and their hardy ponies.

To read the above list bestirs one's blood something after the sound of the pibroch.

A more rapid summary may show the marvelous intellectual and moral force of the men made possible by the life of our Reformer.

POETS.—Drummond, Ramsay, Burns, Thomson, Beattie, Scott, Campbell, Pollok, Lockhart, Montgomery, Wilson, Aytoun.

HISTORIANS.—Buchanan, Burnet, Hume, Robertson, Russell, Watson, Alison, Carlyle.

PHILOSOPHERS.—Adam Smith, Reid, Kames, Stewart, Brown, Sir William Hamilton.

SCIENCE.—Napier, Ferguson, Watt, Playfair, Maclaurin, Leslie, David Brewster, Hugh Miller, Sir Charles Lyell, Sir Roderick Murchison.

Take the Scotch out of the British Scientific Association to-day, and but a small fragment is left.

WRITERS.—Boswell, Smollett, Mackenzie, Blair, McCrie, Chalmers, Jeffrey, Brougham.

TRAVELERS.—Bruce, Park, Ross, Livingstone.

BIBLICAL SCHOLARS.—Too many to mention, while to-day the bodyguard and advanced column toward the very core of the Christian faith is Scotch.

Has there broken forth such a stream of missionary enthusiasm from any other part of the world?

Only to mention Alexander Duff, whose little school in Calcutta grew in thirty-six years to three thousand. And Robert Morrison who captured the language of the Chinaman and taught it to speak the language of the Bible. John Kenneth McKenzie, the Scotch Canadian, and James Gilmore, the apostle to Mongolia; George Leslie Mackay of Highland ancestry, the conqueror of Formosa. To mention Livingstone is to see Africa emerge on the eyes of the world. Melville B. Cox, the first missionary of the Methodist Episcopal Church to Africa, with a name of Scotch fiber, said, "Though a thousand fall let Africa be redeemed." Bishop William Taylor was thoroughly of the same mold, one of the most picturesque and successful missionaries in history.

We all can join Sir Walter Scott in his patriotic lines:

> " O Caledonia, stern and wild,
>   Meet nurse for a gifted child;
>   Land of brown heath and shaggy wood,
>   Land of the mountain and the flood;
>   Land of my sires! what mortal hand
>   Can e'er untie the filial band
>   That knits me to thy rugged strand?"

Where are the monuments of Knox? Where are they not?

PART IV.

SHAMROCK AND THISTLE.

CHAPTER I.

SHAMROCK AND THISTLE.

THE Scotch-Irish, whence are they? In the north of Ireland is the province of Ulster, equal to about one-fifth of the State of Ohio. A thousand years before Knox's time the Irish went over to Caledonia, and so far subdued its people as to leave their own name, Scotch, upon the land. About thirty years after Knox died, the Scotch, in return, went to Ireland, and planted in Ulster an irrepressible Presbyterian Protestantism, sons of Knox.

Thence came to the American colonies, a hundred years after the settlement of the Puritans in New England and the Cavaliers in Virginia, a flood of immigration, which, entering New England, Pennsylvania, and the Carolinas, broke through the Alleghanies into all the West. Following the "Antrim evacuations" in 1704, thirty thousand emigrated to America in two years.

For a long time they were busy in the work of settlement and subjugation of the soil. They helped in the Revolutionary War and the founding of the American Government, silent as to their nationality; but in later years, largely through the organization of the Scotch-Irish Congress in 1889, they have spoken out, made themselves known, and asserted their claims. In this they have resembled very much the floods that break from the mountains of Scotland beneath their snow and ice. It takes time to thaw, but when they break forth, they sweep all before them.

Puritanism is very loosely defined. It was pervasive, and included Protestantism in England, Scotland, Ireland, Holland, and their successors in America. "In England it produced statesmen like Hampden, soldiers like Cromwell, poets like Milton, preachers like Howe, theologians like Owen, dreamers like Bunyan, hymnists like Watts, and saints like Baxter;" in America, Bradford, Cotton, Endicott, Winthrop, Williams.

There is some risk of these Scotch-Irish discounting Yankee Puritanism in their sweeping claims for having accomplished almost all in bringing the country to its present achievements. However, Puritans, having first had their say, can well afford to listen to this broad-shouldered, big-brained, hardy race of Scotch-Irish. In their revolt they dropped the English Rose from the triple emblem, leaving only the Thistle and the Shamrock.

THE DECLARATION OF AMERICAN INDEPENDENCE IS A MEMORIAL.

In Wooster County, Massachusetts, as early as 1773, there were fifty families from Scotland who declared against the domination of the mother country, while the Mechlenburg Declaration in North Carolina came in 1775. When in Independence Hall, July 4, 1776, there was hesitancy about signing the Declaration, Dr. Witherspoon, a lineal descendant of John Knox, said, "To hesitate at this moment is to consent to our slavery. That noble instrument on your table should be subscribed this very moment by every pen in this house. He that will not respond to its accents and strain every nerve to carry into effect its provisions, is unworthy the name of free man, and although these gray hairs must soon descend into the sepulcher, I would infinitely rather that they should descend thither by the hand of the executioner than desert at this crisis the sacred cause of my country." When in a day or two the signing took place, down went the signatures of fourteen Scotchmen.   Like the stone of Scone beneath the coronation chair in Westminster Abbey, the hardy Scot was never removed from his loyalty to the British throne.   Gladstone, with Scotch blood in his veins, practically effected the disestablishment in Ireland, and unhappy Erin has come to her emancipation from a long, intolerable landlordism.

.When, under the new Constitution, also signed by twelve Scots, Washington formed his first Cabinet, he called Alexander Hamilton to the Treasury; Thomas Jefferson, Secretary of State; General Knox, Secretary of War; Randolph, Attorney-General; Rutledge, Wilson, Blair, and Iredell, Associate Justices,—Scotch blood in every one of them. Half of his generals in the Revolutionary War were Scotch. .

In the conquest of the West, David Crockett, Scotch-Irish, pushed out of Tennessee into Texas, and perished at Fort Alamo.   Daniel Boone, of the same race, was the forerunner of civilization in Kentucky, passing thence into Missouri, where he died.

Simon Kenton forced his way savagely into Ohio, and afterward joined George Rogers Clark.   These were the breakers on the wave of Western civilization. Then followed the ruling type of the same Scotch-Irish. Into Texas went General Sam Houston; into Kentucky and northward into Ohio and the Northwest, pre-empting it for the American, George Rogers Clark was sent by Patrick Henry. Still other grades of the same people followed: in Tennessee, Andrew Jackson; in the central parts came Breckenridge, and later Benton; and north of the Ohio, Arthur St. Clair, Anthony Wayne, and Mc-Arthur; followed later by the McDonalds and the McCooks. Francis McCormick, lay preacher, planted Methodism on the Miami over a hundred years ago. Still later to this heart of the Republic came James K. Polk.

Again we must enter the Scotch verdict. Some of their orators claim James Madison, others have claimed Abraham Lincoln. We do not wonder at this, he was so marked by the traits of their nationality. But Nicolay traces him through seven generations of English. Another of their orators even claims Governor Corwin—"Tom Corwin, the Wagoner Boy;" he was unsurpassed in the witchery of his oratory; but was likely English or Hungarian, or both. Should they claim the merry-faced

9

man of the moon, we could only reply "Not proven."
That stately great man who financiered the Republic through our Civil War, Salmon P. Chase, and
Mark Hanna, who could carry a Presidential campaign without campaign speeches, were both
Scotch-Irish. There is on the maternal side a strain
of this blood in Theodore Roosevelt. Never was
there a manlier Presidential campaign than when
two gifted Scotch-Irish, Christian men headed the
Republican and the Democratic tickets in the persons of William McKinley and William J. Bryan.
Forty colonial governors sent to this country before
1776, and twelve Presidents of the United States up
to date, have been of this blood. This book is written in sight of the cemetery where lies the dust of
two Scotch-Irish Ohio governors, Duncan Mc-
Arthur and William Allen.

THEY HAVE BEEN ILLUSTRIOUS IN LAW AND JURISPRUDENCE.

To name John Marshall is but to suggest a line
of such; as, Thomas Ewing, "Salt-boiler" and
"Nestor;" John McLean, Jeremiah S. Black, David
Davis, Allen G. Thurman; Benjamin Harrison, dis-
tinguished as President, more eminent as lawyer;
William C. Preston, of South Carolina, orator and

senator; Attorney-General Crittenden, John G. Carlisle, and Proctor Knott—all great lawyers; Thomas Scott, secretary of the first Constitutional Convention of Ohio, and Supreme Judge; and William T. McClintick, a cultured, gifted lawyer, jurist, and Christian, an honor to his State and to Chillicothe, Ohio, where his life was spent.

ORATORS.

The list were too long to call. Patrick Henry, by his eloquence, decided and precipitated the Revolutionary war. Samuel Galloway, of Columbus, Ohio, was by name, temperament, and electrical eloquence, joined with piety and love of the Scriptures, thoroughly Scotch-Irish. When President Lincoln introduced him to General McClellan, he remarked, "I want to present my friend, Sam Galloway; there is but one of his kind." In the face of the coming Civil War, at a great anti-Nebraska Convention held in Columbus, Galloway was making an address, during which he shouted "Mene, Mene, Tekel, Upharsin!" It seemed to us as though Daniel had come again to judgment. More than any other man he brought the school system of Ohio to order.

PULPIT.

To eliminate this race from the ranks of American preachers were to rob it of much of its glory in Canada and the United States. To specify were a long, invidious task. Part of its emphasis may be seen in its contribution to Methodism as well as to Presbyterianism and the other Churches. It gave such as Mackenzie, McTyeire, Maffitt, Axley, McGee, Cartwright, and Lakin. It has furnished the episcopacy of the Methodist Episcopal Church with a Simpson and a Thoburn. Were the Fitzes and Macs, with all that strain of blood, to be superannuated an immediate election would become necessary to repair the wreck of the episcopal wheel.

This race is capable of great religious enthusiasm, even to wildfire. A pair of Scotch-Irish brothers, Presbyterian and Methodist, John and William McGee, were humanly responsible for the great revival which occurred in 1800, known as the Canebrake Camp-meeting in Kentucky. It was attended with convulsions, jerks, contortions, and other unexplained and inexplicable phenomena, while out of it originated that noble, evangelical Cumberland Presbyterian Church as well as the modern camp-meeting, an institution now largely void of its original power. Ethics and entertainment have taken the place of conversion. Alexander Campbell displayed his Scottish talent and temperament in his protest against all creeds, specially in his own Presbyterian Church. He carried on his battle with an aggressiveness worthy of Knox, until to-day his followers amount to a million and a quarter. This Church dislikes to be called by the name of its founder, preferring that of Disciples of Christ. In truth it has become more softened into a Christian denomination with a fraternal spirit.

EDUCATORS.

In this the Scotch-Irish have greatly distinguished themselves. Blair founded William and Mary for "the glory of Almighty God." It received a land grant before Harvard. There were the Tennents and Witherspoons, McCosh of Princeton, and the late William R. Harper, of Chicago University. The Ohio University, though started by New England Puritans, has had in the line of her presidents several descendants from Ulster. The portraits of Wilson and Howard are Scotchy. McGuffey, who did so much for the literary taste of young America by his school-readers, must have been Scotch-Irish. It is certain that President William H. Scott inherited his stalwart manhood, high moral tone, religious conscientiousness, and philosophical acumen from the North of Ireland on both the paternal and maternal side. Dr. George R. Crooks, of Drew Seminary, scholar and biographer, was of this stock. Some of the chief places in Johns Hopkins and the University of Pennsylvania are filled with Scotch-Irish. Asa Gray, whom I saw in the Rocky Mountains vie with Sir Joseph Hooker in original botany, was of this blood.

JOURNALISM.

In journalism the race has excelled. As editors of newspapers, John Campbell started the *Boston News Letter* in 1704; the first north of the Ohio River, in Cincinnati, 1792, was published by William Maxwell; *The Western Herald*, by James Wilson, was begun at Steubenville, Ohio, in 1806. Horace Greeley and his successor, Whitelaw Reid, in the *Tribune*, furnished fine specimens of talent; and we may add Grady, of the *Atlanta Constitution;* Watterson, of the *Louisville Courier Journal;* James Gordon Bennett, Simon Cameron, with Charles Hammond, of Ohio, in 1812. After him follow the McLeans, Richard Smith, Murat Halstead, Joseph Medill, Samuel Medary; James Scott in Chicago, editor of the *Western Star* at Lebanon, Ohio, and author of Scott's Law taxing the liquor-traffic in his State.

McClure in Philadelphia, and Cockerill; J. B. McCullagh, of the St. Louis *Globe-Demorcat;* John Frew, *Wheeling Intelligencer;* John Russell Young, General Stedman; Bonner, of the *New York Ledger,* are noted; the writer's home, Chillicothe, has one daily, that was edited by a red-hot Scotch-Irishman, William H. Hunter, who has recently died, and to whose courtesy the author is much indebted; and another, G. W. C. Perry, of the stock of Oliver Hazard Perry, whose great "Lake Erie Victory" hangs in the rotunda of the Buckeye Capitol as a fine painting.

When we advance to the realm of magazine literature, we should find that greatly depleted if we take away the Macs from the list of publishers' and editors' names. Daniel Curry was a giant of this race.

We should prejudice our case by ignoring the constellation of brilliant historians, novelists, poets, theological writers, metaphysicians, and scientists, which broke forth from New England Puritanism. In this they led off; but we can not ignore the stream of Scotch-Irish talent. In divinity, Alexander and Hodge are claimed by this race; so is McCosh. Dr. McClintock, of the great Cyclopedia, a man of all-round talent, was Scotch-Irish.

In history, Washington Irving is a name to conjure with, and Douglas Campbell, of multitudinous name, has changed the angle of vision in his "Puritanism in Holland, England, and America."

INVENTORS.

As one hearkens to the puff of the engine, it seems to be shouting the name of "Watt," "Watt," "Watt!" If we listen to the muffled sound of the steamboat, it will speak the name of another Scotch-Irishman, "Robert Fulton," "Robert Fulton," "Robert Fulton!"

Do you hear the singing of the wires overhead? Their melodious note hums the name of another of this race, "Samuel Morse," "Samuel Morse," "Samuel Morse!"

When the trolley-line carries one swinging up and down our valleys, he may hear the name of a man with a Dutch father and a Scotch mother, as it sings "Edison," "Edison," "Edison!"

Should there come ringing on your ear the telephone, hearken well and you will hear the name of a man born in Edinburgh, born again in Boston, saying "Bell," "Bell," "Bell!"

Look at the harvester rolling across the fields, and you will hear it singing its inventor's praise, "McCormick," "McCormick," "McCormick!"

When you roll along a prepared highway in carriage or automobile, you can not forget that the Macadamized way is whispering a Scotchman's name, "Macadam," "Macadam," "Macadam!"

Old Scotia, too, has furnished naval heroes. Jean Paul Jones, with his *Bon Homme Richard*, was Scotch. His bones were lately brought from France to rest under the Stars and Stripes. Oliver Hazard Perry, in his conquering fleet on Lake Erie, had a vessel named *Caledonia*. His Scotch-Irish blood was from his mother, whose grandfather was a Wallace.

The wonder is that these Protestants and lovers of liberty could have adopted slavery. The signers of the Mecklenburg Declaration sowed the Carolinas with slaves. They produced a Calhoun; then pushed their armies against the Republic under the Lees, Morgans, and Kilpatricks. A President of the United States named Buchanan had opened the way, and he was a Scotch-Irishman. One of their orators said, "They kept the commandments and all they could lay their hands on besides." They first acquired their own liberty and then that of their neighbors.

If in this list omissions occur, it is because of the great multitude of illustrious people of Scotch descent and the impossibility of exhausting the roll. What more flat than the oft-used phrase "and others?" It generally falls from the flatterer's pen or that of the impolite. In the present case both motives are denied, and yet I hardly hope to be forgiven. I have not said everything about everybody. But no writer ever did, or ever will.

CHAPTER II.

OUR HERO.

"Having done all to stand."

"Athanasius contra mundum."

WITH many men this may be conviction diluted with stubbornness, or it may be stubbornness fortified by conviction. It may be the heroism of blindness or enlightenment accepting all the risks.

Wellington had given an order to a subordinate. With pale countenance the officer rode away to execute the order. "There," said the great commander, "is a brave man; he sees the danger and faces it." Such was the heroism of our Reformer.

Impetuosity is on the border of sin. So is lethargy.

Mankind admire a moral hero; few seem ready to imitate him. Most of us approve of advancement until it disturbs us. Old usage, however, is not immortal. Even dynamite is better than eternal slumber. Degeneration is easier than regeneration; it is better that great moral forces be guided than resisted. There are times when evil is so entrenched that the only thing left is to bombard the fortress.

We must not discount modern heroism. There is often harmful delusion in asserting that "the former days were better than these." This may be quoted with a whine followed by a yawn.

When the American Civil War came on, there was a wail through the land declaring that there were no George Washingtons or Thomas Jeffersons, no Daniel Websters or General Scotts, but the occasion found the men needed.

Our heroic forefathers did not so miserably fail as to leave no heroic posterity.

Nor may we ignore the superiority of manhood over material conditions whether four hundred years ago or four hundred years hence, whether in John Knox or the man who shall celebrate the communion in Lhassa.

The smartness which considers itself "up to date" discounting the fathers, had as well be modest. Knox never rode an automobile. Luther never called up the Pope by telephone. Elijah did not travel to Mount Horeb on the through limited. Moses never rode in an airship. Millions of moderns are doing these things and yet remain Lilliputians.

By Patient Continuance.

The life of Knox might have seemed wrecked by delays unavoidable.

He was forty-two, nine years beyond the age at which Alexander the Great had conquered the world, before he entered on his life work. Bacon had written his celebrated essays at thirty-six. Savonarola had sent his congregations home, bewailing their sins as they went through the streets, when but thirty-eight. George Whitefield was stirring the hearts of men on both continents at an age when Knox was yet in obscurity. Coming out of his silence at the age of forty-two, could he have seen it, there were but twenty-five years left for his life work. Two of those years were wrested from him by the French galleys. Edward the Sixth called him to England where five years due to Scotland were subtracted. Banished to the continent, over a year was apparently wasted amid the quibbles of a temporary pastorate in Frankfort. Then Geneva took out about four years more, leaving but thirteen for the direct work of the Reformation of Scotland, the completest of all the reforms of that century.

A re-survey of this loss of time may be encouraging. His seventeen years at school in Haddington, his college days at Glasgow, his study of logic and Plato under John Major gave time for his moral and intellectual nature to take root. He learned the power of prayer more perfectly while a galley-slave. After that, in touch with court life and the English under Edward the Sixth, he was himself in training. While in Dieppe ringing out his trumpet blast against the iniquities in England and Scotland, through all these he was forging the sword that cut Scotland free.

REMOTER HEROES.

View him in the light of some Reformers of an earlier day. Saint Cyprian, of Carthagena, in the middle of the third century, spent his force mainly on the non-christian world and lost his head. Knox spent his strength on both papal and secular surroundings, but kept his head—the more is the wonder.

Athanasius, of Alexandria, in the fourth century spent twenty years in exile, but did more for the world with his pen during that banishment than he likely could have done at home. He left as his monument a great confession of faith. Knox left a creed, a kirk, and a new born nation.

Both Cyprian and Athanasius were Bishops. Knox declined that office and so stands out among the rarities of mankind.

Augustine, another white African of the fourth century, transferred his thought through John Calvin into a milder fatalism taught by Knox. But he fell away during his youthful days from the faith taught him by his Christian mother. For John Knox, one conversion was enough.

Chrysostom of the fourth century, a Greek, was golden mouthed. Knox sounded a trumpet, else he might have failed in his work of reform. The Greek was sentenced to banishment for too much plainness of speech, even in his mellifluous periods. A revolt among his Antioch followers and a timely earthquake kept him at home for a time. Queen Eudoxia, however, was like Mary Queen of Scots, and must be rid of the preacher or else reform. In that case Chrysostom had to go. Knox did not go for he would not.

Hildebrand began as a reformer within the Church, but turned out to be Pope Gregory the

Seventh, reputed the most talented of the papal line. Like all reforms within the papal Church, his failed. He did succeed in excluding the nobles and the German Emperor from any part in choosing or investing the Pope. He thus compacted and centralized the power within the papacy, which overshadowed and controlled Scotland in the time of Knox. Knox broke that power and brought Scotland to its feet.

Peter the Hermit, of the latter part of the eleventh century, was a monk and therefore lacked the advice of a wife and the influence of a home to restrain him. He fired the peasant heart and the adventurer's greed so as to lead as many as thirty thousand people through a fatal march of starvation and slaughter for the capture of the Holy Land from the grasp of the Turk.

Knox inspired a crusale against vice within the papal Church and among the Scotch people and won his campaign with the sword of the Spirit.

CHAPTER III.

ELEMENTS OF CHARACTER.

He Was Born Again.

It is well for us that the Christian world is never tired of turning back to the great event in a Christian leader's life when he passed from death unto life consciously. Though not always revealed clearly to the subject himself as a sudden event, yet it is of tremendous importance to all men.

Saul of Tarsus in Damascus breaking into light, the conscious "warming of heart" of Wesley, and the "sweet burning of heart" of Jonathan Edwards, seem more directly matters of consciousness.

Martin Luther emphasizes less the inner change, but hears the voice as if from heaven, "The just shall live by faith."

While the experience of John Knox is largely unrecorded as to how he passed the boundary line from the righteousness of the confessional to that of him whose sole confessor is Christ, we know he had that witness, "We have passed from death unto life because we love the brethren." His heart went out to George Wishart and all like him. Little matter to us now how and when it occurred, but he "first cast anchor" within the ocean of Divine love.

Surely he had been born again. November 9, 1572, he was stricken with his last illness. He lingered for fifteen days. Except one or two conflicts with Satan, he was cheerful and happy. He greatly relished the sixteenth chapter of 1 Corinthians, on the Resurrection of the Dead, remarking, "Is not that a comfortable chapter?"

Once he said, "Now for the last I commend my soul, spirit, and body into Thy hands, O Lord." After repeating the Lord's Prayer he said, "Who can pronounce so holy words?" Later he asked his wife to read John xvii, "Where I cast my first anchor." His watchers had been praying, and inquired of him, "Heard you the prayers?" He answered, "Would to God that you and all men heard them as I have; I praise God for that heavenly sound;" then he said, "Now it is come."

Richard Bannatyne, sitting by him, said, "That we may understand that you hear us, make some sign." He lifted up one hand, and so fell on sleep. That hand was his flag of triumph, saying, "O

Death, where is thy sting? O Grave, where is thy victory? Thanks be to God who giveth us our victory through our Lord Jesus Christ."

ELIJAH.

Like all great, stormy natures, he had his juniper-tree when he sighed to be released from battle. He was a stern self-accuser.

He belonged to those men whose greatness is characterized by self-depreciation. There is danger of this running to excess. It is true of a chain that it is only as strong as its weakest link, but this is not so of a man. With him the stronger parts ought to reinforce the weaker. Conscience may be reinforced by knowledge. Faith will reassure the other so-called links. Hope under the command of will, may pull a man away from under the Juniper-tree, or out of a descending basket by the wall of Damascus or away from the depression of the French galley or from the bed of a paralytic in Edinburgh.

Here are excerpts from his writings:

"The lack of fervency in reproving sin, indifference in feeding those that were hungry, the lack of diligence in execution of mine office, deserved damnation. And besides these I was assaulted—

yea, infected and corrupted—with more gross sin; that is, my wicked nature desired the favors, the estimation, and praise of men; and so privily and crafty did they enter into my breast that I could not perceive myself to be wounded till vainglory had almost got the upper hand.

"Pride and ambition assault me,—on the one part covetousness and malice trouble me; on the other, briefly, O Lord, the afflictions of the flesh do almost suppress the operation of the spirit. I take Thee, O Lord, who only knowest the secrets of hearts to record in none of the aforesaid do I delight. Thou hast sealed into my heart remission of sins received by the blood of Jesus Christ once shed; my manifold rebellions are defaced, my grievous sins purged, and my soul made the tabernacle of Thy godly majesty."

He had a stroke of apoplexy near two years before his death. He overdrew his vitality. Did he not need athletics? He wrote: "By counsel of carnal friends I spared the body, spent some time in taking recreation, and pastime by exercise of body." In a letter he speaks of being "weary of this old carcass." He went so far during his last illness as to order his coffin made. But ere the end came he installed James Lawson, vice-principal of the University of Aberdeen, as his successor over the Church of St. Giles. This gave him great satisfaction.

But Elijah was as good a man under the juniper as on Carmel at the sacrifice; as sincere though mistaken as when Horeb was wrapped in the triple garment of storm, earthquake, and fire.

His chariot and whirlwind were ready when needed, as well as when he was on his way to Hermon nine hundred years later, to a conference with Moses and Jesus about the crucifixion.

Others besides Knox himself have been his detractors; but they knew him not personally, and lived in a world so remote from him as to be incapable of understanding him. Richard Bannatyne lived with him and could not be deceived. His head was too clear and his judgment too cool to be swept away by grief at the death of Knox. Let him speak: "The man of God; the light of Scotland; the comfort of the Kirk within the same; the mirror of godliness, and a pattern to all true ministers in purity of life, soundness of doctrine, and boldness in reproof of wickedness."

This becomes the honest opinion of careful students of history as the years go by, and such he shows up the four hundredth year after he was born.

HIS COURAGE.

This we have seen in all his career. One of the main incentives for writing this book was to add, if possible, a new emphasis to this quality. When Knox had died, Earl Morton, a very talented man, not religious, morally perverse, but a great leader, stood by his grave and gave utterance to a eulogy which has rung on through the centuries, and shall never die out: "Here lieth a man who never feared the face of man." This is an epitaph worth while. Let it be the war-cry of our country till it sweep through the nations. Knox had physical courage; he only fled to Germany from Bloody Mary under the pressure of his friends. When chained to the oar as a galley-slave, he rebuked his keepers without fear, so that in the time of storm the captain, though a papist, asked for Knox's prayers. When he came back from his exile to Scotland and proposed to preach in the Cathedral of St. Andrews, and the archbishop declared he would order the soldiers to fire on him, his friends advised him not to venture; but he did preach there three days in succession so as to rally the officers and the people to set up the reform of worship in that old cathedral town. It took the higher type of courage when he

dissented from English ritualism at Frankfort;
when he sounded his first blast of the trumpet
against Bloody Mary and others; when he rebuked
Gardiner, the Bishop of Winchester; when he confronted Mary, Queen of Scots, and rebuked her
from the pulpit with great courage, afterwards doing the same to her face. At last he sent a message
to Charles IX by his own ambassador, then present
in the audience, warning him of the judgment to
come. And, as he himself foretold, "the ages to
come will be compelled to bear their witness to the
truth." "He never feared the face of man."

HIS POWER IN PRAYER.

The attraction which started this book we have
left till the last,—the reputed prayer of Knox,
"Give me Scotland or I die." This is quoted in the
pulpit and in books on prayer, and has done great
service. Being of such importance, we have sought
to verify it, but in vain. Search has been made personally through a wide range of literature. Correspondence has been had with a dozen of the most
expert in library research in this country, England,
and Scotland, but the frank acknowledgment has
come from every one of them, "I am unable to
verify the prayer." The names of these corre-

spondents would be astonishing. Still, the author believes that Knox gave expression to it. We find in his writing such similar sentiments as these: "The long thirst of my wretched heart is gratified in abundance above my expectation;" "Jesus Christ shall triumph here in the North and the extreme parts of the earth;" "Notwithstanding the fever has vexed me, yet have I traveled through most parts of this realm, where men of all sorts and conditions embrace the truth." In his sixty-seventh and last year he wrote: "Weary of the world, and thirsting to depart;" "I thirst for an end before I be more troublesome to the faithful;" "Now, Lord, put an end to my miserie;" "As the world is wearie of me, so am I of it;" "John Knox, with my dead hand but glaid heart, praising God."

I believe John Knox uttered the cry, for it was in harmony with his entire career as a self-forgetful, self-sacrificing reformer, to pray, "Give me Scotland or I die." Let it fly over the world. It is the heart of the great evangel. It was identical in spirit with the feeling of a man whom Knox so greatly resembled, who wrote, "I could wish myself anathema for my brethren according to the flesh." It sprang from a sublimer source heard on the cross, "Father, forgive them, for they know not what they do."

INDEX